The People's Bible Teachings

TRINITY

One God, Three Persons

Richard D. Balge

NORTHWESTERN PUBLISHING HOUSE
Milwaukee, Wisconsin

Library of Congress Control Number: 00-093125
Northwestern Publishing House
1250 N. 113th St., Milwaukee, WI 53226-3284
© 2001 by Northwestern Publishing House
http://www.nph.net
Published 2001
Printed in the United States of America
ISBN 0-8100-1275-8

Table of Contents

Editor's Preface

The People's Bible Teachings is a series of books on all of the main doctrinal teachings of the Bible.

Following the pattern set by The People's Bible series, these books are written especially for laypeople. Theological terms, when used, are explained in everyday language so that people can understand them. The authors show how Christian doctrine is drawn directly from clear passages of Scripture and then how those doctrines apply to people's faith and life. Most importantly, these books show how every teaching of Scripture points to Christ, our only Savior.

The authors of The People's Bible Teachings are parish pastors and professors who have had years of experience teaching the Bible. They are men of scholarship and practical insight.

We take this opportunity to express our gratitude to Professor Leroy Dobberstein of Wisconsin Lutheran Seminary, Mequon, Wisconsin, and Professor Thomas Nass of Martin Luther College, New Ulm, Minnesota, for serving as consultants for this series. Their insights and assistance have been invaluable.

We pray that the Lord will use these volumes to help his people grow in their faith, knowledge, and understanding of his saving teachings, which he has revealed to us in the Bible. To God alone be the glory.

Curtis A. Jahn
Series Editor

Introduction

At Fountain Abbey in the north of England, medieval monks heard a sermon from their abbot on every Sunday of the year except one. On Trinity Sunday there was no sermon, "owing to the difficulty of the subject."

The doctrine of the Trinity *is* difficult. It is an attempt to say about God what the Bible says about God, not more and not less. We cannot prove that God is three in one, but we can show that the Scriptures teach that he is. It is possible to show that a particular way of trying to express the truth about God is mistaken. It is certainly not possible to prove that the words *Trinity, being, person,* and *nature* are necessarily the only, or the best, ones to express the scriptural truths about God. So far, however, no one has found more useful language.

We cannot accurately define God because the Bible does not define him. We cannot fully comprehend him. God has revealed himself, but he has not told us the truth about himself to the extent that he knows it. A god who fits into my intelligence would be smaller than I am and therefore not God. We can only imperfectly express the truth concerning who God is.

We can, however, (though always imperfectly) describe God on the basis of what he tells us about himself in the Bible. Most important, we can read about what God has done to save every sinner. In his written Word, he tells us what we need to know for our salvation. From the Scriptures we can begin to comprehend what he has done, is doing, and will do for us.

It is just in telling the story of the world's redemption that the Bible tells us that God is one *and* that he is Father, Son, and Holy Spirit. We cannot understand this in terms of arithmetic. We must simply set all mathematics aside and listen to what God says about himself in Scripture. We must use our reason to try to understand what Scripture says, not to decide whether what Scripture says is reasonable or true.

The doctrine of the Trinity is inseparably linked to the truth that Jesus Christ is our divine Savior. It is therefore a practical doctrine, not a marginal teaching on the "fringe" of what is important to our faith. Friedrich Schleiermacher (1768–1834) has been called "the father of modern theology" and "the founder of modern Protestant theology." In his book of systematic theology *The Christian Faith*, this German rationalist treated the doctrine of the Trinity in an appendix! Since he did not believe that Christ is the eternal God who became fully human for our sake, and because he regarded the Holy Spirit as simply the church's "common spirit,"[1] he did not know what to do with the doctrine of the Trinity. Since Schleiermacher, "modern theology" has generally dismissed the doctrine as false, outdated, or irrelevant. It is not surprising that "modern theology" has also dismissed the Bible's teaching about Christ's incarnation and his atonement for sin. As we shall see, those doctrines are inseparably connected with the doctrine of the Trinity.

In this book we will answer the questions, "Can God be known?" and "How can God be known?" Then we will look at what the Bible teaches about God the Father, God the Son, and God the Holy Spirit. We will trace the story of how teachers of the early church attempted to put these truths into words. We will see that even Bible-believing

Christians of considerable intelligence had great difficulty finding the right concepts and language. We will see that some more recent theologians, teaching and writing on this doctrine, have merely revived and restated ancient errors. With regret and sorrow, we will point out the ways in which various religions deny and oppose the Bible's teachings and how some Christian sects have erred in expressing the doctrine of the Trinity. Finally, we will see how the great trinitarian creeds came into existence, and we will examine them briefly.

As a result of our study, we hope to be drawn closer to the true God, so that we might "fear, love, and trust in [him] above all things" (Luther's Small Catechism).

1

Can God Be Known, and How?

Only God *really* knows God. No one has eyewitness information to offer regarding him. He "lives in unapproachable light," and "no one has seen or can see" him (1 Timothy 6:16). The wisest philosopher has no advantage over the ordinary person in this matter. "For who among men knows the thoughts of a man except the man's spirit within him? In the same way no one knows the thoughts of God except the Spirit of God" (1 Corinthians 2:11). Just as you and I cannot know each other's inmost thoughts (we often do not understand our own thoughts!), so we cannot, with our limited human intelligence, know God's thoughts or comprehend who he really is.

Revealed in nature

The Bible was not written to prove that there is a God. In its very first words, it assumes his existence and his activity: "In the beginning God created the heavens and the earth" (Genesis 1:1). There is no discussion of whether there is a God or what God is like. The author simply makes God the subject of the first sentence and begins to speak about what God has done. The Bible can do that because God has revealed himself in the natural world and in the inner nature of human beings.

Although he has not revealed his essential being or all his thoughts, God has made himself known in nature and continues to do so. True, he cannot be confined in a test tube or scrutinized under a microscope. He has, however, revealed a great deal about what he is like, what he has done, and what he is doing. He has revealed himself as the Creator and the judge in what we call natural law, in the human conscience, and in history. He has not, however, revealed himself in nature as the Savior.

Creation

Paul writes in Romans 1:19,20: "What may be known about God is plain to them [the Gentiles, or heathen], because God has made it plain to them. For since the creation of the world God's invisible qualities—his eternal power and divine nature—have been clearly seen, being understood from what has been made, so that men are without excuse." Since the first day of creation, the vastness of the universe, the marvels of the human body and mind, and the infinite variety of nature have cried out "God made us!" David declares in Psalm 19:1, "The heavens declare the glory of God; the skies proclaim the work of his hands."

The world that we can see, which fills us with awe, testifies that only an eternally powerful and wise divine being could be responsible for this amazing world. "It didn't happen by itself" has always been man's instinctive reaction, although we know that this natural knowledge can be suppressed by the incessant drumming of atheistic evolutionary theory as fact.

What God reveals about himself in creation does not depend on the insights of genius or even on the lifelong study of science. Without help from philosophers or scientists, ordinary people recognize that there must be a power behind the way this world came into being and underlying the ways in which it is preserved. Many who understand higher mathematics and science marvel at the evidence of a designer in nature. The most primitive tribes sense the presence of a divine power. God "has not left himself without testimony: He has shown kindness by giving you rain from heaven and crops in their seasons; he provides you with plenty of food and fills your hearts with joy" (Acts 14:17). Knowing that there is a god, but not knowing who he is, they worship man-made gods or the spirits of creatures, hoping to gain their favor or appease their wrath. It is really more natural to believe in God's existence than to disbelieve.

Natural law

Before Adam and Eve sinned, they had obeyed God's law perfectly. Because their fall into sin affected every human being that would ever be born, our knowledge of right and wrong is blurred and imperfect. Still, though human beings are by nature utterly corrupted by sin, even the heathen "know God's righteous decree that those who do such things deserve death" (Romans 1:32). "Such things" are listed in the catalog of sins against God and our fellow human beings that Paul provides in Romans 1:18-31. That catalog includes gross idolatry, homosexuality, murder, and less spectacular sins that are not always recognized or acknowledged as sins—such as envy, gossip, arrogant boasting, and disobedience to parents.

How do sinners know about "God's righteous decree" (Romans 1:32)? In a parenthetical comment at Romans 2:14,15, Paul speaks of God's law written in the hearts of those who do not know the Ten Commandments: "Indeed, when Gentiles, who do not have the law, do by nature things required by the law, they are a law for themselves, even though they do not have the law, since they show that the requirements of the law are written on their hearts, their consciences also bearing witness, and their thoughts now accusing, now even defending them." The apostle is not saying that the heathen (Gentiles) keep the law to God's satisfaction. They are, however, doing some of the things required by the law. We might say they have some understanding that it is wrong to dishonor parents, murder, take a neighbor's spouse, steal, or harm another person's reputation. The natural corruption of sin and many generations of sinners have blurred this law written in people's hearts. It is there, however, and it bears witness that we must answer to our Maker for how we live. People can have some of this knowledge brainwashed out of them by unbelieving teachers or by atheistic literature. Unless they are really perverse, however, they realize that they are accountable to God, the giver of the gift of life.

Conscience
The Gentiles, said Paul, who do not have the written law but do have the law written in their hearts, also have

consciences, "their consciences also bearing witness, and their thoughts now accusing, now even defending them" (Romans 2:15). Conscience is the "inner voice," given by God to every human being, that reminds sinners of what is moral and what is immoral. Conscience testifies to the rightness or wrongness of what we have done. Conscience rightly accuses the wrongdoer, and it defends the person who does what is right. Unless it is smothered or cauterized or completely warped, conscience is there to tell even the non-Christian that right is right and wrong is wrong.

History

God has also revealed his preserving and governing presence in the history of the world—even in the lives of individuals. From the day he spoke the word of blessing to Adam and Eve, "Be fruitful and increase in number; fill the earth and subdue it. Rule over the fish of the sea and the birds of the air and over every living creature that moves on the ground" (Genesis 1:28), to this day, God has directed and controlled the destinies of nations. He has determined how long any civilization will endure. He has set the boundaries for every nation and empire. "From one man he made every nation of men, that they should inhabit the whole earth; and he determined the times set for them and the exact places where they should live" (Acts 17:26). Empires rise and fall according to his will. He orders the course of civilizations and cultures, the geography and history of nations. We cannot usually interpret his acts (especially while they are in progress) or explain why he orders events as he does, but history has demonstrated again and again that he is in charge.

Purpose of God's revelation in nature

For what purpose does God reveal himself in nature and in the testimony of conscience to natural law? As we see in Paul's address before the assembly of the Areopagus (Mars' Hill) in Athens, it is to move people to seek the true God: "God did this so that men would seek him and perhaps reach out for him and find him, though he is not far from each one of us" (Acts 17:27). The fact of our existence and the resources for living that God provides should prompt us to seek the giver of all good gifts. God demonstrated his power and intelligence in creation and in the history of nations so that people would realize an intelligent and powerful being is in charge of the universe. In God's intention this should make them seek him, reach for him, and try to find him. The people who dedicated an altar "TO AN UNKNOWN GOD" in Athens (Acts 17:23) had sought and they were reaching, but they had not yet found.

God's revelation in nature leaves sinners "without excuse" (Romans 1:20). More important, it provides points of contact for the revelation of God in his Son, Jesus Christ, for the gospel that God has revealed in the Bible.

The folly of atheism

If God has revealed his power in creating the universe, his goodness in preserving it, and his wisdom in governing it, how can anyone deny that he exists? How can an unbelieving astronomer say, "The heavens do *not* declare the glory of God, and the skies do *not* show the work of his hands"? Only by stubbornly denying the evidence do they suppress the truth by their wickedness (Romans 1:18). Not intelligence but wickedness causes people to deny and disobey God. People cannot use the excuse that they don't know about God's existence. Atheists are not atheists by nature but because they reject the testimony of nature. They do not deny God because they are more intelligent than other people are, but because of their own corruption. "The fool says in his heart, 'There is no God.' They are corrupt, their deeds are vile; there is no one who does good" (Psalm 14:1).

Atheistic theories of evolution have led many people to deny nature's testimony of God. One Christian writer makes this observation:

> In his *Descent of Man*, Darwin made clear that he did not believe that conscience or moral sense came from God. . . . Darwin denied that man has an instinctive belief in God. . . . It should not surprise us that Darwin's followers would take his teachings to their inevitable conclusions. If evolution were true, there would be no need for an almighty, all-knowing God, no need for a supernatural Creator. And if there were no God, there would be no supernatural Being to whom we must answer. There would be no absolute right or wrong, since moral standards also would be a result of evolution, changeable and flexible. Sin would be an idea from which man must be liberated. The Savior himself would be unnecessary. Man would have no purpose on earth other than to live for himself and his own glory. In spite of the dreary picture just painted, most people today accept the theory of evolution as an accurate account of man's origin.[2]

The trap of self-righteousness

Adherents of many world religions, even those who profess to believe in one god, seek to gain God's acceptance and favor by what they do and how they live. We are thinking here of the work-righteousness of Judaism and Islam in particular. Both insist that God is one, but both also depend on their own deeds to gain God's favor.

The number of Muslims (adherents of Islam, who worship Allah and do not want to be called Muhammadans) is rapidly increasing in North America. Buddhists venerate the Lord Buddha but do not believe in a personal god. Buddhism, especially Zen Buddhism, is growing in influence in the Western world.

Adherents of the New Age Movement quote the Bible when it suits their purposes, but they reject the God of the Bible and emphasize their own supposed inborn divinity.

More than natural knowledge is needed

The natural knowledge of God does not enable anyone to do what pleases God. The law written in human hearts makes it possible for families, communities, and civilizations to function in an orderly and relatively peaceful manner. The natural knowledge of God, however, does not make people love God or enable them to keep his law. On the one hand, sinners can suppress the natural law and conscience in order to do what they simply want to do. Their sinful nature can assert itself against God and his will. On the other hand, sinners can conform in an outward way to the Golden Rule, but without love for God or trust in him.

Most important, the natural knowledge of God does not show people their Savior. That leaves people, in their natural state, under God's wrath: "The wrath of God is being revealed from heaven against all the godlessness and wickedness of men who suppress the truth by their wickedness" (Romans 1:18). It makes them subject to "God's righteous decree that those who do such things deserve death" (Romans 1:32). Lacking the fear and love of God in their hearts, "they not only continue to do these very things but also approve of those who practice them" (Romans 1:32).

God revealed in his Son, Jesus Christ

The evangelist John writes, "No one has ever seen God, but God the One and Only, who is at the Father's side, has made him known" (John 1:18). Jesus, the Word of God who became flesh (John 1:14), has made God known. The Greek word used in John 1:18 for "has made him known" could also be translated as "interpreted," "explained," or "described." What we need to know about God, we know in and from his Son, Jesus Christ.

Jesus said, "All things have been committed to me by my Father. No one knows the Son except the Father, and no one knows the Father except the Son and those to whom the Son chooses to reveal him" (Matthew 11:27). What even Moses, who saw only God's back (Exodus 33:18-23), could not do, the Son of God has done. Jesus has seen the Father, known the Father, and reveals the Father. As God's Son, Jesus is witness to all the Father's intentions toward the human race. As true man, he speaks in a language we can understand when he tells us what those intentions are.

God revealed in Scripture

The true God is known in Jesus Christ. All that we can know about Jesus Christ, we know from the Bible. The revelation of God in his Son and the revelation of God in the Scripture are not independent of each other or different from each other. Christ is the heart and core of Scripture, and Scripture bears witness to Christ. To those who challenged his claim to be the Son of God and his authority to teach as he did, Jesus said: "You diligently study the

Scriptures because you think that by them you possess eternal life. These are the Scriptures that testify about me. If you believed Moses, you would believe me, for he wrote about me" (John 5:39,46). The prophecies, the promises, the ceremonies and sacrifices—indeed, all Old Testament history—testified about Christ. His conception and birth, his life of service, his death and resurrection were all fore-told and foreshadowed in the Old Testament. The New Testament was written to bear witness to him and what he did: "These are written that you may believe that Jesus is the Christ, the Son of God, and that by believing you may have life in his name" (John 20:31).

The Bible does not answer every serious question we might ask or satisfy every curiosity we might have. It does, however, make us wise for salvation and equip us to serve our Savior-God. As Paul wrote to Timothy: "From infancy you have known the holy Scriptures, which are able to make you wise for salvation through faith in Christ Jesus. All Scripture is God-breathed and is useful for teaching, rebuking, correcting and training in righteousness, so that the man of God may be thoroughly equipped for every good work" (2 Timothy 3:15-17). "The man of God," inci-dentally, does not mean the pastor. It means the Christian. Scripture equips every Christian "for every good work."

The Holy Scriptures are the only reliable source from which we can learn who God is, what he does, and what he has in mind for us. It is fashionable in some circles to say, "I trust Christ, not the Bible. My faith is in the Savior, not in a book." Fashionable, but deceptive. How can any-one trust Jesus without trusting the only authentic and reliable source of knowledge about him? On the other hand, what hope and comfort would the Scriptures give us if it were not for their message of Christ the Savior?

2

I Believe in God

The name of God

In Romans 10:13,14, Paul writes: "'Everyone who calls on the name of the Lord will be saved.' How, then, can they call on the one they have not believed in? And how can they believe in the one of whom they have not heard? And how can they hear without someone preaching to them?" We cannot trust a human being we only know exists but do not really know. By the same token, we could not trust a god we did not know, if we only knew of his existence. Thank God, he does make himself known by telling us his name. His name tells us what he is like, what he has done, and what he is doing. In terms of Paul's words in Romans 10:13,14, someone has preached his name to us so that we could hear. That message has enabled us to trust him and thus to be saved.

In the previous paragraph, we find Paul calling God "the Lord" (Romans 10:13). The Bible also refers to him as "the Father" and "the Almighty." God is known by many other proper names in Scripture. God's name stands for who he is and what he does and what he wants us to know about him. He does this through Jesus, the Word who became flesh. He also does it in his written Word, the Bible. In the upper room on the night before his crucifixion, Jesus prayed to his Father for his disciples. He said, "Now this is eternal life: that they may know you, the only true God, and Jesus Christ, whom you have sent. I have revealed you [in Greek: revealed *your name*] to those whom you gave me out of the world. They were yours; you gave them to me and they have obeyed your word. For I gave them the words you gave me and they accepted them. They knew with certainty that I came from you, and they believed that you sent me" (John 17:3,6,8). God tells us his name so that through it we may be saved: "This is eternal life" (verse 3).

God tells us his name and the meaning of his name in the book of Exodus. From the burning bush in the wilderness, "God said to Moses, 'I AM WHO I AM.' This is what you are to say to the Israelites: 'I AM has sent me to you'" (Exodus 3:14). God is a personal being who speaks and acts. He is not a mere impersonal power in nature. He is not "the Force" of *Star Wars*. Without beginning and without end, GOD IS. There was a time when you and I—and this whole world—did not exist. Unless Jesus returns before we die, it will be said of us, "They were." God, however, *is*, without beginning and without end, constant and unchangeable. God's special Old Testament name Yahweh (Jehovah) is based on the Hebrew word for "I AM" of Exodus 3:14. In our English Bibles, this name, in translation, is frequently spelled with four capital letters, the first one large and the other three smaller: LORD. That name always reminds us that he is the God of free and faithful grace, who keeps his promises. He was not elected, and he cannot be impeached or deposed. He simply is.

After God delivered the Israelites from Egypt, after he gave them the law at Mount Sinai, after Moses pleaded with the Lord to have mercy on the calf-worshiping people, God appeared to Moses again, proclaiming his name: "Then the LORD came down in the cloud and stood there with him and proclaimed his name, the LORD. And he passed in front of Moses, proclaiming, 'The LORD, the LORD, the compassionate and gracious God, slow to anger, abounding in love and faithfulness, maintaining love to thousands, and forgiving wickedness, rebellion and sin. Yet he does not leave the guilty unpunished; he punishes the children and their children for the sin of the fathers to the third and fourth generation'" (Exodus 34:5-7).

We might say that God preached a complete sermon in those words, with the threats of the law and the gracious assurance of the gospel. He declared that he is faithful in his compassion, grace, patience, and forgiveness. He is also faithful to himself, to his own character, in punishing those who despise him and disobey his commandments: "He does not leave the guilty unpunished."

Later in Israel's history, he said: "I the LORD do not change. So you, O descendants of Jacob, are not destroyed" (Malachi 3:6). His very name sets him apart from every god that humans might fashion or imagine. He still reveals that name to us and, thus, reveals himself to us through the preaching of the law and gospel.

It is of great significance that the name the LORD in the original Hebrew of the Old Testament is always translated as *kyrios* (KEY-ree-us) in the Greek translation of the Old Testament. In the Greek New Testament, the word *kyrios* (Lord) is used in reference to Jesus more than 150 times. In Romans chapter 10, Paul equates confessing that Jesus is Lord with calling on Yahweh of the Old Testament. In verse 9 he writes, "If you confess with your mouth, 'Jesus is Lord,' and believe in your heart that God raised him from the dead, you will be saved." In verse 13 Paul quotes the first words of Joel 2:32: "Everyone who calls on the name of the LORD will be saved." Thus he identifies Jesus in the New Testament with Yahweh of the Old Testament.

The attributes of God

The Bible does not define God. God has not revealed his absolute being, his essence, to us. The Bible does, however, reveal God's attributes (his characteristics), and by these we know him. We learn who he is by learning what he is like. We cannot comprehend God's essence, and so he reveals himself by his attributes, in words we can understand. We usually make a distinction between the attributes and the essence of a thing. In the case of God, however, his attributes describe his very essence (being). For example, it is not only an attribute of God that he loves. *"God is love"* (1 John 4:8).

Many of God's attributes, especially his justice, would only terrify and doom us if it were not for his attribute of grace. He is everywhere; sinners cannot hide from him. He knows all things; sinners cannot fool him. He is all-powerful; sinners cannot escape his wrath. He is holy; we are not. These are messages of law that warn and terrify us.

But the central message of the Bible is that God for Christ's sake has forgiven all sinners. For a believer who enjoys the forgiveness of sins in Christ, these same attributes now give gospel comfort. Because God is everywhere, we will never travel beyond his loving care. Because God knows all things, he knows our troubles and needs. Because God is all-powerful, he can defeat all our enemies.

At this point let us take a brief look at some of the attributes of God. We will see later that these characteristics describe not only the Father but the Son and the Holy Spirit as well. If the Son and the Holy Spirit have the same attributes as the Father, they also have the same divine essence (being) as the Father. Knowing about these attributes affects our faith and lives. What we know and believe about God makes a difference in time as well as for eternity.

The God of free and faithful grace is *eternal*, without beginning and without end, completely independent of time. In his farewell blessing to Israel, Moses assured the people, "The eternal God is your refuge, and underneath are the everlasting arms" (Deuteronomy 33:27). As God preserves and protects you and me and all his creatures, as he listens to the prayers of all his children, God is never pressed for time. The clock and the calendar never limit him in what he can do. For him, it is always now, and he doesn't need to put off anything until later. "See, the former things have taken place, and new things I declare; before they spring into being I announce them to you" (Isaiah 42:9). The eternal God will never die and leave us to our own devices in the universe, never retire and leave us looking for a replacement, never get tired and leave us on our own.

God is *omnipresent*, everywhere at once. When we are tempted, we sometimes need the reminder that there is no place where God is not: "'Can anyone hide in secret places so that I cannot see him?' declares the LORD. 'Do not I fill heaven and earth?' declares the LORD" (Jeremiah 23:24).

In the day of trouble, it is good to know that God is *almighty*, all-powerful: "When Abram was ninety-nine years old, the LORD appeared to him and said, 'I am God Almighty; walk before me and be blameless'" (Genesis 17:1). Abram was hard pressed, and he needed reassurance. Almost 25 years had passed since God first promised that Abram would have a son, and from that son's descendants, the Savior of the world would come. Abram was now 99 years old and Sarai, his wife, was just 10 years younger. There was, humanly speaking, no possibility that they would ever have a child. With the announcement "I am God Almighty," the Lord was reminding Abram that the laws of nature do not bind the ruler of nature. God is powerful to preserve and protect, to make everything in his creation serve his gracious purposes. God would demonstrate that in Abram's life with the birth of his son Isaac.

If we ever imagine that our secret sins are unknown to God, we are shocked back to reality by the reminder that God knows all things. He is *omniscient*, as Solomon acknowledged in his prayer at the dedication of the temple: "Deal with each man according to all he does, since you know his heart (for you alone know the hearts of all men)" (1 Kings 8:39). But these words are also a comfort as much as they are a warning, aren't they? As believers, we are happy that our loving God knows all about our difficulties and heartaches.

God is *holy*. He said to Moses, "Speak to the entire assembly of Israel and say to them: 'Be holy because I, the LORD your God, am holy'" (Leviticus 19:2). God is just, perfect in his works, as well as faithful: "He is the Rock, his works are perfect, and all his ways are just. A faithful God who does no wrong, upright and just is he" (Deuteronomy 32:4).

God is *compassionate*: "The LORD is good to all; he has compassion on all he has made" (Psalm 145:9).

God is *love*. He provides for the needs of all, whether they love him or not: "He causes his sun to rise on the evil and the good, and sends rain on the righteous and the unrighteous" (Matthew 5:45). The highest expression of his love was to bring about the salvation of sinners. Paul wrote to the Romans, "God demonstrates his own love for us in this: While we were still sinners, Christ died for us" (5:8). God does not love us because we are lovable or because our actions are lovely—or because we love him. He loves us because he is love. John writes: "This is how God showed his love among us: He sent his one and only Son into the world that we might live through him. This is love: not that we loved God, but that he loved us and sent his Son as an atoning sacrifice for our sins" (1 John 4:9,10). There could be no greater demonstration that God is love. John adds in verse 11: "Dear friends, since God so loved us, we also ought to love one another."

I believe *means "I trust"*

Faith is more than believing that God exists. James writes: "You believe that there is one God. Good! Even the demons believe that—and shudder" (James 2:19). It is possible to know and say all the correct things about God and yet not believe in God in the biblical sense.

I believe in God means more than "I know his name and his attributes." *I believe in God* means "I trust God and rely on his Word." To believe is to trust, to rely, to stake all on what (whom!) I trust. Believing in God's one and only Son does not mean loving my neighbor as myself. I have not lived up to that. Believing is not experiencing the "Inner Light," feeling something like an electrical shock, or making a decision for Christ. Nor is it merely assenting to a dogma. It is relying on Jesus Christ, who was obedient in life and death as the substitute for every human being, whom God raised from the dead as the beginning of a great crop of people who will be raised to everlasting life.

Strictly speaking, it is not faith that saves us; it's the Savior. It is not faith that justifies; it's God. Faith only trusts that he has done it. In that sense we are justified through faith. Without the cross, without the empty tomb, without the Savior obediently living and dying for us, faith would have no foundation. When a lifeguard throws a life ring to a drowning person, that person does not concentrate on the strength of his grip. He focuses on the life ring. So faith does not examine itself, measure itself, rely on itself. It focuses on Christ, who is strong to save. Do not ask "Do I have faith?" Rather, ask "Do I have a Savior?" The answer to the first question is yes when we know that the answer to the second question is yes.

In this regard, Martin Luther says, "Even if my faith is feeble, I still have the selfsame treasure and the selfsame Christ that others have. There is no difference."[3]

Abraham is remembered as the "father of all who believe" (Romans 4:11). When he was about one hundred years old, when his wife Sarah was well beyond child-bearing age, God renewed his promise of a son and many descendants for Abram: "No longer will you be called Abram; your name will be Abraham, for I have made you a father of many nations" (Genesis 17:5). Humanly speaking, it seemed such a promise could never be fulfilled. Why hadn't God made good on his promise years before? "Yet he [Abram] did not waver through unbelief regarding the promise of God, but was strengthened in his faith and gave glory to God, being fully persuaded that God had power to do what he had promised" (Romans 4:20,21). Faith is relying on the promises of God, in which he has revealed himself as the Savior. Faith is taking the trustworthy God at his trustworthy word. Faith is not merely "I believe that . . ." It is, especially, "I trust in . . ."

Faith is the beggar's hand that receives the gift of eternal life. It is not something we produce or generate. It is God's gift. "For it is by grace you have been saved, through faith—and this not from yourselves, it is the gift of God—not by works, so that no one can boast" (Ephesians 2:8,9). By God's grace and through faith, we have been saved. Like grace, faith is the gift of God. Faith is not a self-produced decision to accept God's salvation. Just as we did not decide to accept physical life from our parents but simply received it as a gift, so the spiritual life of faith is a gift, not the result of a decision made by our own power.

God gives faith by means of his Word: "Faith comes from hearing the message, and the message is heard through the word of Christ" (Romans 10:17). Ultimately, it is not our act of hearing but the words of Christ that work faith. Faith is generated by the Holy Spirit: "I tell you that no one who is speaking by the Spirit of God says, 'Jesus be cursed,' and no one can say, 'Jesus is Lord,' except by the Holy Spirit" (1 Corinthians 12:3).

God gave us faith and forgiveness in Holy Baptism. He nourishes and strengthens our faith with the assurance of forgiveness in Christ's Supper. He continues to do these things daily through his Word.

3

The Father and the Son Are God

The Father is God

Creator of all that is

That the Father is God has rarely been questioned or disputed within the Christian church. He is acknowledged as the almighty Maker of all things, visible and invisible. This does not mean that the Son and the Holy Spirit were not involved in the creation of the universe. We will speak of their involvement in chapter 7. Scripture, however, associates the work of creation with the Father in particular. We speak of creation as the Father's special, or particular, work.

Father of our Lord Jesus Christ

"Praise be to the God and Father of our Lord Jesus Christ! In his great mercy he has given us new birth into a living hope through the resurrection of Jesus Christ from the dead" (1 Peter 1:3). When many and various religions speak of God as the Father but do not acknowledge his Son as equally divine with him, they dishonor both Father and Son. They are left with a god who is an idol, not God. Jesus said, "He who does not honor the Son does not honor the Father, who sent him" (John 5:23). As we shall see in chapter 5, according to his divine nature, Jesus Christ is God's Son from eternity and in their relationship to each other, the Father is eternally his Father. The Scripture passages that identify Jesus Christ as the Son of God are also affirming that the Father is a person distinct from the Son.

There would seem to be one exception to the statement made in the first sentence of this chapter. There is a large and fast-growing sect known as the Oneness Pentecostals. The word *Oneness* signifies that these people believe there is only one person in the Godhead, not three. That person, they say, is Jesus. The Father and the Holy Spirit are only other names for Jesus. They point to John 10:30, where Jesus says, "I and the Father are one." Doesn't the word *are* already suggest two persons and not just one person? More important, Greek, like many other languages, uses different forms of a word to denote masculine, feminine, or neuter gender. The word for *one* in John 10:30 is neuter. Thus, Jesus is saying, "The Father and I are one being; we have an essential unity." *One* is not masculine: "The Father and I are one and the same person." The same verse, by the way, can be used to rebut those who, like Jehovah's Witnesses, regard the Son as subordinate to the Father, a sort of secondary god. As the Athanasian Creed puts it: "Each person—the Father, the Son, and the Holy Spirit—is distinct, but the deity of Father, Son, and Holy Spirit is one, equal in glory and coeternal in majesty."[4]

The Oneness Pentecostal sect (also called Unity Pentecostals) especially likes to use Isaiah 9:6 as a proof text: "For to us a child is born, to us a son is given, and the government will be on his shoulders. And he will be called Wonderful Counselor, Mighty God, Everlasting Father, Prince of Peace."

Since this is a prophecy concerning Jesus the Messiah, they see the phrase *Everlasting Father* and conclude that Jesus is the same person as the Father. What Isaiah's prophecy is actually saying is that the Messiah would be a loving and benevolent guardian looking out for the best interests of his people—as a human father does. Jesus exercises all the loving care of the God who preserves and saves us, but he is not the first person of the Trinity.

The Father of those who believe in Jesus

The risen Christ sent this message to his brothers: "I am returning to my Father and your Father, to my God and your God" (John 20:17). How was it that Jesus' brothers have God as their Father? How can we confidently address him as Father? Paul writes, "You are all sons of God through faith in Christ Jesus" (Galatians 3:26). "Sons," of course, includes daughters, whom God honors by addressing them with the same word he uses for his one and only Son. In contradiction to Oneness Pentecostalism, this verse makes clear that there is a distinction between Father and Son, that Father and Son are not the same person.

Those who believe in a fatherhood of God and brother-hood of man apart from Jesus sometimes quote the prophet Malachi: "Have we not all one Father? Did not one God create us? Why do we profane the covenant of our fathers by breaking faith with one another?" (Malachi 2:10). People seem to overlook the prophet's third question, "Why do we profane the covenant of our fathers?" Malachi was rebuking his fellow Jews for marrying heathen women. He was not arguing that those women and their families were all God's children. He was saying the opposite.

The Son is God

It is impossible to discuss the doctrine of the Trinity without paying particular attention to the truth that in Jesus Christ the second person of the Trinity became fully human. Indeed, apart from this truth, we would not know about or be interested in the doctrine of the Trinity. This truth was the point of contention in the great controversies over the Trinity in the fourth century. Controversy over the person of Christ, especially his divine nature, moved and stimulated the church to formulate the Apostles' Creed, the Nicene Creed, and the Athanasian Creed. Certain words and phrases in these creeds not only express positive truths about Christ but also identify and reject errors.

Truly human

An early error concerning Jesus denied that he was truly human. Various individuals and groups held a "docetic" (doe-SEE-tick) view of him. That is, they taught that Jesus only "seemed" (in Latin: *docet*, DOE-ket = seems) to be a flesh and blood human being. Many of these Docetists considered the material and physical world to be essentially evil. They refused to believe that the pure and holy Son of

God assumed a physical body. They regarded him as a sort of phantom. Others even denied that he really died, some suggesting that Simon of Cyrene died in his place.

Those who deny the doctrine of the Trinity today do not question Jesus' humanity. As has usually been the case throughout the two thousand years since he came to this earth, their problem is with his divinity. Of course, some of those who refuse to take the Bible at face value say we cannot really know anything about him. In that sense they too are really denying his humanity.

Although it will not be necessary for our purposes to treat the true humanity of Christ at great length, let us briefly review the scriptural evidence. The Bible clearly presents a Jesus who is truly human in every respect but one: he was without sin. "For we do not have a high priest who is unable to sympathize with our weaknesses, but we have one who has been tempted in every way, just as we are—yet was without sin" (Hebrews 4:15). He was born of a woman in order to be subject to the law (Galatians 4:4). Hebrews 7:26 describes him as "holy," not polluted by sin; "blameless," free from every kind of evil; "pure," not stained by any transgression. He is "set apart from sinners," not aloof from our human struggles but not partaking in our sinful attitudes and actions. That he measured up to God's law in every respect is evident from the fact that he is "exalted above the heavens."

He came into the world as a helpless baby (Luke 2:12). He was a descendant of King David (Romans 1:3). He developed physically, mentally, and spiritually, growing and learning (Luke 2:40). He was hungry (Matthew 4:2). He slept (Matthew 8:24). He wept (John 11:35). He was overwhelmed with sorrow (Matthew 26:38). He was thirsty (John 19:28).

Jesus Christ not only shared in our humanity. In order to complete his saving work he even accepted our mortality. As we confess in the Apostles' Creed, "he was crucified, died, and was buried" (see Mark 15:24,37,46). He had to be human to die in our place and save us from the devil's grip: "Since the children have flesh and blood, he too shared in their humanity so that by his death he might destroy him who holds the power of death—that is, the devil—and free those who all their lives were held in slavery by their fear of death" (Hebrews 2:14,15).

Martin Luther puts it this way:

> We Christians should know that if God is not in the scale to give it weight, we, on our side, sink to the ground. I mean it this way: if it cannot be said that God died for us, but only a man, we are lost; but if God's death and a dead God lie in the balance, his side goes down and ours goes up like a light and empty scale. . . . *But he could not sit on the scale unless he had become a man like us, so that it could be called God's dying, God's martyrdom, God's blood, and God's death. For God in his own nature cannot die; but now that God and man are united in one person, it is called God's death when the man dies who is one substance or one person with God* [emphasis added].[5]

In taking on our human nature and in obeying God's law to the full, the Son of God subjected himself to death. He did that for a special and glorious purpose. He has put the devil, "who holds the power of death" (Hebrews 2:14), out of commission. Jesus, who shared in our humanity, has neutralized the devil's ultimate weapon by dying. He did this by satisfying God's justice and paying the price of our deliverance. The devil still exists and people still die, but death has lost its power to terrify us who trust the Savior.

Truly God

In order to take our place under the demands and penalties of God's law, to redeem us, the Son of God became man. To actually accomplish this, to set us free from sin and Satan, to accomplish our salvation, he needed to be God as well. The best efforts of the best man could never have saved the world.

When God's Son became fully human, he did not cease to be what he had been from eternity—divine. Paul exhorted the elders of the church at Ephesus: "Keep watch over yourselves and all the flock of which the Holy Spirit has made you overseers. Be shepherds of the church of God, which he bought with his own blood" (Acts 20:28). The expression "his [God's] own blood" reminds us that when God became man, he did not stop being God. As the God-man he was not two persons but one. What the man did, God did. When Jesus' blood was shed, God's blood was shed. *God* bought the church with his own blood. As Athanasius of Alexandria (d. A.D. 373) reminded the heretic Arius and his followers again and again, redemption is God's work. In insisting on that, Athanasius was not being a mere hairsplitter or fussy theologian. He was safeguarding the truth of our salvation.

Divine works and attributes

The New Testament says that the second person of the Trinity was actually involved in various divine works from the beginning, long before he appeared as the babe of Bethlehem. "Through him all things were made; without him nothing was made that has been made" (John 1:3). The uncreated Son of God, the eternal Word, played a role in the creation of the universe. Without his activity, there would have been no universe. Paul says the same

thing in Colossians 1:16: "For by him all things were created: things in heaven and on earth, visible and invisible,
whether thrones or powers or rulers or authorities; all
things were created by him and for him."

The Son of God, who was present and active when all
things were made, also holds all things together by his
powerful word: "The Son is the radiance of God's glory
and the exact representation of his being, sustaining all
things by his powerful word" (Hebrews 1:3). "His powerful
word" brought all things into existence and it still preserves them. His power "enables him to bring everything
under his control" (Philippians 3:21).

During his ministry, Jesus demonstrated his divine
power and his other attributes in many miracles. He who
created the winds and the waves and established the laws
of nature "rebuked the winds and the waves, and it was
completely calm" (Matthew 8:26). The Lord exercised his
divine power by sending a band of demons into a herd of
pigs (Mark 5:11-13).

When he healed a paralytic (Luke 5:17-26), Jesus
demonstrated his divine omniscience and his divine
omnipotence as well as his divine grace:

> **Omniscience:** He saw the faith of the paralyzed
> man's friends and recognized that the paralyzed
> man's deeper problem was the need for forgive-
> ness: "When Jesus saw their faith, he said,
> 'Friend, your sins are forgiven'" (Luke 5:20).
> He also knew what the Pharisees and the
> teachers of the law thought about someone
> who claimed authority to forgive sins: "The
> Pharisees and the teachers of the law began
> thinking to themselves, 'Who is this fellow

who speaks blasphemy? Who can forgive sins but God alone?' Jesus knew what they were thinking and asked, 'Why are you thinking these things in your hearts?'" (Luke 5:21,22).

Omnipotence: He used his almighty power to heal the man: "'Which is easier: to say, "Your sins are forgiven," or to say, "Get up and walk"? But that you may know that the Son of Man has authority on earth to forgive sins. . . .' He said to the paralyzed man, 'I tell you, get up, take your mat and go home.' Immediately he stood up in front of them, took what he had been lying on and went home praising God" (Luke 5:23-25).

Divine grace: Most important, Jesus graciously used his divine authority to forgive sins.

All of this demonstrated that he is God.

Jesus demonstrated his divine power and grace in raising Jairus' daughter (Matthew 9:18-26; Mark 5:22-43; Luke 8:41-56), the young man of Nain (Luke 7:11-16), and his dear friend Lazarus (John 11:38-44) from the dead. Jesus himself "through the Spirit of holiness was declared with power to be the Son of God by his resurrection from the dead" (Romans 1:4). On the Last Day, he, "by the power that enables him to bring everything under his control, will transform our lowly bodies so that they will be like his glorious body" (Philippians 3:21). He himself rose, and he will raise us. What sin and death have spoiled and corrupted, he will change into something splendid and immortal.

"For Christ died for sins once for all, the righteous for the unrighteous, to bring you to God. He was put to death in the body but made alive by the Spirit, through whom also he went and preached to the spirits in prison" (1 Peter 3:18,19). Not to suffer, not to preach the gospel, but to proclaim his victory over Satan, Christ descended into hell ("prison"). To all the inhabitants of hell, he cried out the news of his triumph. Satan was leading a great victory party because Jesus had been crucified, had died, and was buried. The devil thought the second Adam was defeated and that God's great rescue of sinners had been frustrated. And then the triumphant Son of God appeared, and the party in hell was over.

Paul expresses much the same thought in his letter to the Colossians (2:15). Using the image of a Roman general's triumphal procession, he says the defeated armies of hell are publicly shamed by Christ's victory: "And having disarmed the powers and authorities, he made a public spectacle of them, triumphing over them by the cross." The "powers and authorities" are the conquered demons. The cross seemed to clinch their final victory over God, but it turned out that Christ was "triumphing over them by the cross."

Jesus overcame Satan's temptations in the wilderness, won many victories over demons in his ministry, and struck the final killing blow against the devil by his death on the cross. God confirmed that in Christ's resurrection. God exalted the Savior by raising him from the dead, and in so doing, he also gave us new life and hope: "Praise be to the God and Father of our Lord Jesus Christ! In his great mercy he has given us new birth into a living hope through the resurrection of Jesus Christ from the dead" (1 Peter 1:3).

God is the final judge of every human being. The Father has committed that divine office to the Son. Jesus said, "The Father judges no one, but has entrusted all judgment to the Son" (John 5:22). Paul writes, "God will judge men's secrets through Jesus Christ, as my gospel declares" (Romans 2:16). Thus, *God the Son,* who is also true man, is the final judge of every human being.

After Jesus had rebuked the winds and waves and stilled the furious storm on the Sea of Galilee, "The men were amazed and asked, 'What kind of man is this? Even the winds and the waves obey him!'" (Matthew 8:27). Perhaps they were not sure of the answer then, but they learned to trust and confess him as the Son of the Most High, as Lord and God.

Divine names

Nine months before the Savior was born, the angel told Mary: "The Holy Spirit will come upon you, and the power of the Most High will overshadow you. So the holy one to be born will be called the Son of God" (Luke 1:35). The title "Son of God" does not belong to him merely because of his miraculous conception and birth. The title does not simply mean that Jesus was the Messiah either. Rather, it speaks of the Son's eternal relationship to the Father.

To the shepherds of Bethlehem, the Lord's messenger declared, "Today in the town of David a Savior has been born to you; he is Christ the Lord" (Luke 2:11). As we noted earlier, the Greek translation of the Old Testament used the word *kyrios* (KEY-ree-us) in reference to the special Old Testament name of God, "the LORD." The Greek New Testament regularly applies the same title to Jesus, referring to him as "the Lord." Peter, for example, writes, "Praise be to the God and Father of our Lord Jesus Christ!" (1 Peter 1:3). Since Jesus' conception, according to Jesus' human nature, God is Jesus' God. According to

Jesus' divine nature, Jesus is the Lord. In his first epistle, Peter urges us to believe and confess the same truth: "In your hearts set apart Christ as Lord. Always be prepared to give an answer to everyone who asks you to give the reason for the hope that you have. But do this with gentleness and respect" (3:15). As a devout Jew, Peter would never have written such things if he had not believed that Jesus is truly the Lord God.

Pious Jews would not think of deifying a mere human being, but Jesus' Jewish disciples called him "the Son of God," and "the Holy One of God," and he accepted those divine names. "Then those who were in the boat worshiped him, saying, 'Truly you are the Son of God'" (Matthew 14:33). "Simon Peter answered, 'You are the Christ, the Son of the living God'" (Matthew 16:16). "Nathanael declared, 'Rabbi, you are the Son of God; you are the King of Israel'" (John 1:49). "Simon Peter answered him, . . . 'We believe and know that you are the Holy One of God'" (John 6:68,69). After Jesus' resurrection, "Thomas said to him, 'My Lord and my God!'" (John 20:28). Jesus did not repudiate those confessions, as he should and surely would have done if Thomas's words were not true.

The very demons can recognize and must acknowledge that Jesus is divine. The evil spirit that possessed the man who lived in tombs "shouted at the top of his voice, 'What do you want with me, Jesus, Son of the Most High God? Swear to God that you won't torture me!'" (Mark 5:7).

Divine honor

The New Testament also indicates that Jesus is to be worshiped and honored as God. All people should honor the Son, "just as they honor the Father" (John 5:23).

Philippians 2:9-12 says, "Therefore God exalted him [Jesus] to the highest place and gave him the name that is above every name, that at the name of Jesus every knee should bow, in heaven and on earth and under the earth, and every tongue confess that Jesus Christ is Lord, to the glory of God the Father."

When the apostle John saw a glimpse of the glory of heaven, he saw the hosts of heaven praising Jesus along with the Father. John saw ten thousand times ten thousand angels singing, "Worthy is the Lamb, who was slain, to receive power and wealth and wisdom and strength and honor and glory and praise!" (Revelation 5:12). John heard a united chorus of praise to both the Father and Jesus: "To him who sits on the throne and to the Lamb be praise and honor and glory and power, for ever and ever!" (Revelation 5:13).

Needless to say, if Jesus is worshiped in heaven along with the Father "for ever and ever," he must be true God, equal with the Father.

"All the fullness of the Deity"

There are religious people willing to grant that there was something divine in Christ. Some say that he received divine characteristics as a special gift or reward from God. Paul says infinitely more than that in Colossians 2:9: "For in Christ all the fullness of the Deity lives in bodily form." That says, "Everything that God is, Christ is." The divine being, all the divine characteristics, all God's authority and power reside in the man Jesus. While he walked the earth, he concealed his deity for the most part, although he did not give it up or lose it. He never ceased to be God. How this can be is beyond comprehension, but it is what God's Word teaches. The Eternal became a baby; the Creator became a creature. The Lord of life laid down his life. God and man are a single person!

When, in Romans 1:3, Paul writes that Christ, "as to his human nature, was a descendant of David," his words imply that Jesus has another nature, the divine. That is what the angel told Mary when he announced the Savior's forthcoming birth: "The Holy Spirit will come upon you, and the power of the Most High will overshadow you. So the holy one to be born will be called the Son of God" (Luke 1:35). He is *called* the Son of God because he *is* the eternal Son of God.

"In the beginning was the Word, and the Word was with God, and the Word was God. He was with God in the beginning. The Word became flesh and made his dwelling among us. We have seen his glory, the glory of the One and Only, who came from the Father, full of grace and truth" (John 1:1,2,14). John does not say merely, "God was *in* the Word." "In the beginning," before the world began, says John, "The Word *was God.*" He is not a demigod, a semideity. From eternity, he has the nature of God and is essentially God.

The Word, who in the beginning was God, became flesh. As we have seen, he became fully human. "Made his dwelling among us" (John 1:14) literally means "pitched his tent with us." He made the earth his temporary dwelling while he accomplished our salvation. He did not cease being God during that time. No, in this one person, the divine nature and the human nature were and continue to be united. That is the sense in which we must understand Jesus' words to Philip. "Philip said, 'Lord, show us the Father and that will be enough for us.' Jesus answered: 'Don't you know me, Philip, even after I have been among you such a long time? Anyone who has seen me has seen the Father. How can you say, "Show us the Father"?'" (John 14:8,9). Jesus and the Father are one not only in love for the world. Jesus and the Father are one in deity. They share in the one divine being. "For in Christ all the fullness of the Deity lives in bodily form" (Colossians 2:9). In the words of the Athanasian Creed: "We believe and confess that our Lord Jesus Christ, God's Son, is both God and man. He is God, eternally begotten from the nature of the Father, and he is man, born in time from the nature of his mother."[6]

4

The Holy Spirit Is God

In the Nicene Creed, the church confesses the Holy Spirit, "who in unity with the Father and the Son is worshiped and glorified."[7] He is called the *Holy* Spirit because he is God and because he is completely separated from any and all *evil* spirits. The Holy Spirit is sometimes called the "shy" person of the Trinity, because he does not call attention to himself. The fact is, it is his business to call attention to the Father and the Son and not to himself. Nevertheless, we do worship and glorify him, because we know from his book that he is actually a person, is identified with God, has the attributes of God, does God's work, and proceeds from the Father and the Son.

Personality

Spirit, or *Ghost,* is the English for the Old Testament (Hebrew) word *ruach* (ROO-akh) and the New Testament (Greek) word *pneuma* (puh-NOI-ma). Both words have the meaning "breath" or "wind." Taking the word literally, the Holy Spirit is the "breath" of God. This, however, does not mean that the Holy Spirit is a mere thing and not a person. As the "breath" of God he is, as the Nicene Creed puts it, "the giver of life."

Scripture speaks of the Holy Spirit as a person. God's Old Testament people "rebelled and grieved his Holy Spirit. So he turned and became their enemy and he himself fought against them" (Isaiah 63:10).

Rebellion and sin grieve the Holy Spirit, as the words of Paul in Ephesians 4:30 also indicate: "And do not grieve the Holy Spirit of God, with whom you were sealed for the day of redemption." A seal is a mark of identification or ownership. Paul says here that the Holy Spirit will identify us on judgment day, "the day of redemption." The Spirit will testify then that we are God's own, bought with Christ's blood, and elected for eternal salvation. Therefore, we are God's possession and welcome in God's eternal kingdom. We surely do not want to vex or grieve this Spirit. Jesus said (Matthew 12:32), "Anyone who speaks a word against the Son of Man will be forgiven, but anyone who speaks against the Holy Spirit will not be forgiven, either in this age or in the age to come." Again we see that the Spirit is not merely a power or emanation from God. As one who can be grieved and sinned against, he is more than God's "self-consciousness" or (as Schleiermacher said) "the spirit of the church."

The Spirit was the agent of Jesus' conception (Matthew 1:18). He was present and active at Christ's baptism, appearing in the form of a dove and anointing Jesus for his ministry as the Messiah (Matthew 3:16). As Isaiah foretold: "The Spirit of the LORD will rest on him—the Spirit of wisdom and of understanding, the Spirit of counsel and of power, the Spirit of knowledge and of the fear of the LORD" (11:2).

The Holy Spirit is involved every time someone is baptized: "[God] saved us, not because of righteous things we had done, but because of his mercy. He saved us through the washing of rebirth and renewal by the Holy Spirit" (Titus 3:5). It would be incongruous to mention him with the Father and the Son in connection with Baptism (Matthew 28:19) and in the apostolic blessing (2 Corinthians 13:14) if he were not a distinct divine person.

Identified as God

Just as Athanasius reminded the church that redemption is divine work and that Christ the Redeemer must therefore be truly God, so Athanasius also taught that the Holy Spirit must be divine in order to unite us with Christ. Furthermore, only if the Holy Spirit is truly God are we justified in worshiping and glorifying him with the Father and the Son.

Recall how Peter accused Ananias of dishonesty for claiming that he and Sapphira had brought the entire proceeds from their sale of real estate to the apostles for distribution to the poor. "Peter said, 'Ananias, how is it that Satan has so filled your heart that you have lied to the Holy Spirit and have kept for yourself some of the money you received for the land? Didn't it belong to you before it was sold? And after it was sold, wasn't the money at your disposal? What made you think of doing such a thing? You have not lied to men but to God'" (Acts 5:3,4). In lying to the Holy Spirit, Ananias had lied to God.

Speaking to those Jews in Rome who refused to believe the gospel of Jesus Christ, Paul referred to Isaiah 6:9 and identified the Holy Spirit as God. Isaiah 6:9 reads: "He [the Lord] said, 'Go and tell this people: "Be ever hearing, but never understanding; be ever seeing, but never perceiving."'"

When Paul, in Acts 28:25,26, uses the words of Isaiah, the apostle makes the Holy Spirit the speaker: "The Holy Spirit spoke the truth to your forefathers when he said through Isaiah the prophet: 'Go to this people and say, "You will be ever hearing but never understanding; you will be ever seeing but never perceiving."'"

Expressing a single truth with parallel thoughts, Paul identifies God with God's Spirit in 1 Corinthians 3:16: "Don't you know that you yourselves are God's temple and that God's Spirit lives in you?" He is saying that the Holy Spirit is God. In 1 Corinthians 12:6,11, speaking of the distribution of spiritual gifts to Christians, the apostle equates the Spirit with God: "There are different kinds of working, but the same God works all of them in all men. All these are the work of one and the same Spirit, and he gives them to each one, just as he determines."

Divine attributes

As true God, the Spirit shares in all the attributes (characteristics) of God. We cite a few reminders of this fact from the Scriptures.

The Spirit is *eternal.* Christ "through the eternal Spirit offered himself unblemished to God" (Hebrews 9:14). The Spirit possesses *divine knowledge,* searching "the deep things of God" (1 Corinthians 2:10). The Spirit is *omni-*

present: "Where can I go from your Spirit? Where can I flee from your presence? If I go up to the heavens, you are there; if I make my bed in the depths, you are there" (Psalm 139:7,8).

Divine works

With the Father and the Son, the Holy Spirit participated in the work of creation, "hovering over the waters" (Genesis 1:2). His creative work continues, as Job's friend Elihu acknowledged: "The Spirit of God has made me; the breath of the Almighty gives me life" (Job 33:4).

All living creatures in each new generation are the products of the Spirit's continuing creative activity: "When you send your Spirit, they are created, and you renew the face of the earth" (Psalm 104:30).

The Holy Spirit was involved in Jesus' work of redemption. We have already mentioned his role in the Savior's conception, and his presence at Christ's baptism. It was the Spirit who led Jesus into the desert to win the threefold victory over the tempter (Matthew 4:1). God promised through Isaiah that the Spirit of the Lord would rest on his Anointed One: "The Spirit of the Sovereign LORD is on me, because the LORD has anointed me to preach good news to the poor. He has sent me to bind up the brokenhearted, to proclaim freedom for the captives and release from darkness for the prisoners" (Isaiah 61:1).

In the synagogue at Nazareth, Jesus read these words and applied them to himself and his proclamation of the gospel: "Today this scripture is fulfilled in your hearing" (Luke 4:21). The Spirit had equipped Jesus for his ministry of salvation.

The Holy Spirit empowered, guided, and inspired Jesus' apostles, as the Savior promised he would. The disciples would be called on to speak under great pressure when they were summoned before the Jewish authorities and when they testified before governors and kings. Jesus encouraged them with the promise that their efforts and the outcome would not really depend on them. The Spirit would do the work: "It will not be you speaking, but the Spirit of your Father speaking through you" (Matthew 10:20). The Spirit testified about Jesus to the apostles, so that they could also testify concerning Jesus: "When the Counselor comes, whom I will send to you from the Father, the Spirit of truth who goes out from the Father, he will testify about me. And you also must testify, for you have been with me from the beginning" (John 15:26,27).

The Savior kept his promise to send the Spirit. The book of Acts records many instances in which fishermen who had little formal learning spoke with an eloquence that came from the Holy Spirit. Peter's sermon on Pentecost (Acts 2:14-40) is an obvious instance. His words before the Sanhedrin (Acts 4:8-12) provide another example of his being "filled with the Holy Spirit."

The Holy Spirit is still involved in the life and work of the church. Indeed, he gives the church life, as he regenerates sinners and makes saints of them. The people of the church are "being built together to become a dwelling in which God lives by his Spirit" (Ephesians 2:22). The Holy Spirit helps us in our prayer life, and he himself intercedes for us. Paul writes to the Romans: "The Spirit helps us in our weakness. We do not know what we ought to pray for, but the Spirit himself intercedes for us with groans that words cannot express" (8:26).

The Spirit distributes gifts to Christ's church: "All these are the work of one and the same Spirit, and he gives them to each one, just as he determines" (1 Corinthians

12:11). When Barnabas and Saul were chosen, called, and sent to preach the gospel in Cyprus and Asia Minor, it was the Spirit who prompted the church to send them: "While they were worshiping the Lord and fasting, the Holy Spirit said, 'Set apart for me Barnabas and Saul for the work to which I have called them.' The two of them, sent on their way by the Holy Spirit, went down to Seleucia and sailed from there to Cyprus" (Acts 13:2,4). In a similar way, the Spirit plays a role in the calling of the church's ministers today, as he did in the calling of the shepherds of the church of God at Ephesus (Acts 20:28): "Keep watch over yourselves and all the flock of which the Holy Spirit has made you overseers. Be shepherds of the church of God, which he bought with his own blood."

Filioque

Filioque (feel-ee-OH-queh) is Latin for "and the Son." It comes from the phrase "who proceeds from the Father *and the Son*" in the Nicene Creed. The expression did not appear in the original (Greek) version of the Nicene Creed. It seems to have been added to the creed by the Synod of Toledo (Spain) in 589. The Frankish church under Charlemagne decided to introduce the phrase into the creed in 809, at the Synod of Aachen. Pope Leo III (d. 816) refused to include it in the creed as used by the church at Rome, but in subsequent years the entire Latin or Western church (including Rome) accepted it. In 867, Patriarch Photius (FOE-shuss) of Constantinople excommunicated Pope Nicholas I of Rome for "corrupting the creed." Although other factors played a role, the *filioque* was the principal theological reason for the Great Schism between the Eastern and Western churches in 1054. Still today, the inclusion of the *filioque* in the Nicene Creed and the doctrine that underlies that wording constitute a significant doctrinal difference between the Eastern Orthodox and Roman Catholic churches.

Filioque was a doctrine of the church long before it became part of the formal creed. In Matthew 10:20, Jesus identifies the Spirit as "the Spirit of your Father." Christians also knew from Scripture that the Holy Spirit is not only the Spirit of the Father but also the Spirit of the Son. In Galatians 4:6, Paul writes: "Because you are sons, God sent the Spirit of his Son into our hearts, the Spirit who calls out, '*Abba*, Father.'" The expression "the Spirit of Jesus" in Acts 16:7 also reminds us that the Spirit proceeds from the Son as well as from the Father: "When they came to the border of Mysia, they tried to enter Bithynia, but the Spirit of Jesus would not allow them to." Consider Paul's words in Philippians 1:19 as well: "I know that through your prayers and the help given by the Spirit of Jesus Christ, what has happened to me will turn out for my deliverance." The little word *of,* in each of the verses quoted in this paragraph, signals that the relationship of the Spirit to the Son is the same as his relationship to the Father. If he proceeds from the Father, as he does, he also proceeds from the Son.

We paraphrase what the great teacher of the Western church, Augustine of Hippo (d. 430), said on this subject: The Son is equal with the Father and shares in all the Father's acts. Therefore, since the Father "spirates" (breathes) the Spirit, so does the Son. Hence the Holy Spirit proceeds from the Son as well as from the Father. Recalling that *ruach* (Hebrew) and *pneuma* (Greek)—the Bible words for spirit—also mean "breath," we can see why theologians chose the concept "spiration" as one way to express the relation of the Spirit to the Father and the Son.

The term *procession* helps us conceive of the relationship between the Spirit and the other two persons. Just as *begotten* says that the Son was "not made," so *proceeding* says that the Spirit was neither made nor created nor begotten. The procession is not a physical process. Nor is it conditioned by time. Because it is eternal, it in no way makes the Holy Spirit "younger" than the Father or the Son. Because the Holy Spirit is God with the Father and the Son, procession in no way makes the Holy Spirit inferior to the other two persons. All three partake equally in the eternal majesty of the one divine being. Like *Trinity, essence, person, begotten,* and other such words, *procession* does not explain or prove anything about God. It mostly says what the Holy Spirit is not—not created, not begotten—and it helps clarify our thinking about his relationship to the Father and the Son.

On the night he was betrayed, at the Last Supper, Jesus said to the Twelve: "When the Counselor comes, whom I will send to you from the Father, the Spirit of truth who goes out from the Father, he will testify about me" (John 15:26). Where our translation reads "goes out" the King James Version reads "proceeds." To avoid possible misunderstanding, we must point out that Jesus does not speak here of the Holy Spirit's eternal procession or going out from himself (Jesus). He speaks of the relationship of the Spirit to the Father—and all such relationships within the Godhead are eternal. When Jesus says "I will send," he is talking about what he (Jesus) will do in future time, not about the eternal relationship between himself and the Spirit.

The ancient hymn of praise, "We Praise You, O God" (Te Deum Laudamus), proclaims the Father, the Son, and the Holy Spirit as God. It is fitting for us to do the same.

Throughout the world the holy Church acclaims you:
Father of majesty unbounded,
your glorious, true, and only Son,
and the Holy Spirit, advocate and guide.[8]

5

Trinity: Terms Used by the Church

From the Bible we know that believers trusted Jesus Christ as their divine Savior long before they joined in confessing their faith in the words of the Apostles' Creed or the Nicene Creed. Christians were filled with the Holy Spirit and worshiped Jesus as God long before they developed the concepts and language with which the doctrine of the Trinity is discussed and defined. Faith does not need learned proof or argumentation, and what is in the heart is always deeper and clearer than mere words can ever express. Early in the church's history, however, doubters—but also some earnest Christian thinkers—began to ask questions such as, "How can there be only one God when the Father is God, the Son is God, and the Holy Spirit is

God?" More often, the questions focused on Jesus: "How could God become a man?" "What is the relationship of the divine nature to the human nature in Christ?"

A practical doctrine

Everything that God says about himself in Scripture—including his self-revelation as Father, Son, and Holy Spirit—commands our interest because he is the God of our salvation. Although the Bible does not present a detailed doctrine of the Trinity, it does show us the Father, Son, and Holy Spirit in action. It presents each person of the Trinity acting for the salvation of human beings. The Father sent his one and only Son into the world to save us. God the Son became one of us, fully human but without sin, to ransom us. God the Holy Spirit testifies to these facts and events, convinces us of the truth of this good news, and thus makes us children of God and heirs of eternal life.

That is what the ancient church set forth in the creeds, especially detailing and emphasizing what the Son did for us and for our salvation. The Formula of Concord, the 1577 confessional writing of the Evangelical Lutheran church, says:

> The entire holy Trinity, God the Father, Son, and Holy Spirit, directs all men to Christ as to the book of life in whom they are to seek the Father's eternal election. For the Father has decreed from eternity that whomever he would save he would save through Christ, as Christ himself says, "No one comes to the Father but by me" (John 14:6), and again, "I am the door; if anyone enters by me, he will be saved" (John 10:9).[9]

Throughout history and today, those who have rejected the doctrine of the Trinity have been people who refuse to believe that Jesus Christ is essentially God. They do not want to acknowledge him as the only mediator between God and man. They have no use for his perfect obedience in our place and on our behalf. Imagining that they can satisfy God's requirements by themselves, they deny the only Savior they will ever have.

Salvation is God's work. The triune God has done the work we could never do for ourselves.

Some helpful language

As we have already noted, the ancient teachers of the church developed and used three terms that are not used in the Bible. They did so in order to express, in as concise and precise a manner as they could, what the Bible teaches about God. The three words are *Trinity, being* (substance or essence), and *person.* We say that God is one divine being, consisting of three persons, the Trinity.

In the second century, beginning with Theophilus of Antioch, various Greek Christian authors used the word *trias* (TREE-ahs) to express the "threeness" of God. Around the year 180, the Greek teacher Athenagoras (accent on the third syllable) wrote something decidedly "trinitarian." What he said is not nearly as clear and complete as the great creeds of the church, in part because the great controversies that helped to shape those creeds were still mostly in the future. Answering the critics' charge that Christians were atheists, Athenagoras wrote: "Who, then, would not be amazed hearing those called atheists who call God Father and Son and Holy Spirit, proclaiming their power in union and in rank their diversity?"[10] *Union* and *diversity* were then and are still important concepts in discussing the God of the Bible.

The North African Latin author Tertullian (150?–222?, accent on the second syllable) provided the oldest sample we have of the word *trinitas* (TRIN-i-tahs), from which our English word *Trinity* comes. He articulated the doctrine of the Trinity in a way that satisfied the Latin or Western church and left the West relatively untroubled by the later Arian controversy (fourth century), in which the eternal deity of the Son was denied. Tertullian taught that God is one "substance" and that in this substance there are three "persons." He had been trained as a lawyer and used legal terms. In Roman law, *substance* meant a single entity, and *person* meant a party to any action having to do with that entity. In God, said Tertullian, there is a single entity (substance, essence, being) and three parties to the action (persons). Unlike some of his contemporaries, Tertullian said that the Son and Spirit did not result from a *division* of the Father, but that they are an *extension* of the Father—like rays from the sun. That is a comparison that Origen (OH-ri-jen) of Alexandria also made.

Origen (185–254) was the brilliant teacher who said, "We recognize that God was always the Father of his only-begotten Son. . . . Wisdom [the Son], therefore, must be believed to have been begotten beyond the limits of any beginning that we can speak of or understand."[11] In other words, if the Father has been the Father eternally (as he has been), he must have had a Son eternally (as he has had). Therefore, the Son is also eternal. Furthermore, said Origen, the Logos (LUG-us = Word), or Son, or second person, did not cease to be divine when he assumed the human nature.

Origen also adopted two philosophical words that the church has found useful in discussing the relation of the divine to the human in Christ. Unfortunately, the church was not ready to adopt them until almost two hundred years after Origen's death. He wrote concerning the Savior: "If it [human understanding] think of a God, it sees a mortal; if it think of a man, it beholds Him returning from the grave. . . . The truth of both natures may be clearly shown to exist in one and the same Being."[12] Today we say, "In Christ, both natures (*physeis*) exist in one and the same person (*hypostasis*)."

In 269, the Synod of Antioch declared that Jesus Christ is the incarnation of the preexistent Logos (Word, see John 1:1-14). Dionysius of Rome confessed that the Son is of the same substance (essence, being) with the Father and is therefore eternally God. In the decades that followed, other theologians made helpful contributions in the long and difficult struggle to express the Scripture truth correctly—or at least to avoid saying what is mistaken and thus harmful.

The word being

One way of explaining what is meant by God's *being* is to say, "It is that something in God by which he is what he is." Being (essence, substance), when used in philosophy—or even in everyday language—is an abstraction, a mere concept without real existence. But when we speak of God, we are speaking of one who eternally and truly *is*. In the words of the Augsburg Confession, "There is one divine essence [being], which is called and which is God."[13]

The word person

When speaking of God, the church uses the word *person* in a sense in which it is not used anywhere else. It is critically necessary to say what the church means and what it does not mean to say with this word. Otherwise we might mistakenly think of three gods. Or, we might imagine that Father, Son, and Holy Spirit are merely qualities or modes of operation or various powers of the one being.

Since we are speaking of God, three *persons* cannot mean three "people." *Persons* does not mean "parts" either. The three persons are not parts of God, for each person is himself God. Article I of the Augsburg Confession puts it this way: "The term 'person' is used, as the ancient Fathers employed it in this connection, to signify not a part or a quality in another but that which subsists of itself."[14] The great mystery of the Trinity is how the three persons are related to one another in one divine being without being mere parts of that being.

The church uses the word *person* in a special way to mean a self-conscious and self-determining ego, a party to the divine action. It means that in God there is an eternal reality that corresponds to what God has revealed about himself (Father, Son, and Holy Spirit) in creating, redeeming, and sanctifying us. Not only has he *revealed* himself as Father, Son, and Holy Spirit; he *is* Father, Son, and Holy Spirit. Jesus himself illustrates this "person-hood." In John 17:6, Jesus says *I* concerning himself and addresses the Father as *you*: "I have revealed you to those whom you gave me out of the world. They were yours; you gave them to me and they have obeyed your word." In John 15:26, Jesus speaks of the Holy Spirit as he, while speaking of himself as I, and referring to the Father as distinct from both the Holy Spirit and himself: "When the Counselor comes, whom I will send to you from the Father, the Spirit of truth who goes out from the Father, he will testify about me."

The word Trinity

As we have seen, the early church coined the word *Trinity* in order to summarize what the Bible teaches about God, to express who God is and what he is like. It is clear that the authors of the New Testament believed that God is one. On the other hand, they also believed that the Father is God, the Son is God, and the Holy Spirit is God.

Building on the teachings of the apostles, teachers of the early church developed and formulated the language for the doctrine of the Trinity. They were not only trying to say what the Scripture says. They were also reacting against the unscriptural language and false ideas of various teachers. In this work the church borrowed some of the language of philosophy. This was partly because abstract terms can be useful in summarizing the Bible's teachings, but especially because false teachers were giving false meanings to the language of Scripture.

The Bible's language is concrete and historical: "The Father did," "Jesus said," "the Spirit sent," "God is." In using abstract Greek terms, the church's teachers did not change the facts of Bible history or make God's truth harder to understand. They did use the educated language of their times to try to present God's Word clearly, to expose error where it appeared, and to avoid making errors themselves. Certain scholars of the 19th century, most notably Adolf von Harnack (1851–1930), charged that the trinitarian doctrine and creeds changed the simple teaching of Jesus and the apostles into a speculative philosophical system. That is not the case. As we have seen and shall see, everything the creeds confess about God, he has revealed about himself in his written Word.

The three ecumenical (universal, confessed by Christians everywhere) creeds—Apostles' Creed, Nicene

Creed, Athanasian Creed—remain as faithful summaries of the Bible's teaching about the Trinity and as safeguards against false teaching in the church. No one has succeeded in improving on them, and those who think they can be dispensed with are ignorant of the church's history. Either they fail to understand what Scripture teaches, or they simply refuse to accept what Scripture teaches.

6

The Trinity: Three Persons

Bishop Hilary of Poitiers (d. 366) said that God is One, but he is not solitary.[15] We speak of three persons in the Godhead. We believe, on the basis of the New Testament, that God sent his Son to redeem the world, that Jesus Christ is God in the flesh, who came to save us, and that the Holy Spirit is he who has given us faith and other spiritual gifts. The three are distinguished each one from the other two.

We have seen where the term *persons* came from and how it came to be used. For now, let us simply repeat that in this special use it does not mean "people" or "beings" or "parts." God is one being, and he cannot be divided into parts. This is not about arithmetic but about what the

Bible teaches concerning God. The great teacher of the Western church, Augustine of Hippo (d. 430), wrote: "Certainly there are three. . . . But when it is asked three what, then the great poverty from which our language suffers becomes apparent. But the formula three persons has been coined, not in order to give a complete explanation by means of it, but in order that we might not be obliged to remain silent."[16]

The Trinity in the New Testament

Probably the most familiar words that speak of the Trinity are those spoken by Jesus as he gave his disciples the Great Commission: "Therefore go and make disciples of all nations, baptizing them in the name of the Father and of the Son and of the Holy Spirit" (Matthew 28:19). We use the words of this "trinitarian formula" at the beginning of worship, in Baptism, when the forgiveness of sins is announced, when the congregation sings "Glory Be to the Father" (Gloria Patri), and when we pray Luther's Morning and Evening Prayers. Each time we do so, we are saying God is one, for Jesus said *name* not *names*. We are also saying that Father, Son, and Holy Spirit are three distinct persons. We are confessing that each is God. The three persons of the Godhead are also enumerated in the familiar apostolic blessing of 2 Corinthians 13:14: "May the grace of the Lord Jesus Christ, and the love of God, and the fellowship of the Holy Spirit be with you all."

The angel Gabriel mentioned all three persons when he announced the coming birth of Mary's Son: "The Holy Spirit will come upon you, and the power of the Most High will overshadow you. So the holy one to be born will be called the Son of God" (Luke 1:35). The Holy Spirit, the Most High, the Son of God—all three persons.

All three persons were also present and manifest at Jesus' baptism: "As soon as Jesus was baptized, he went up out of the water. At that moment heaven was opened, and he saw the Spirit of God descending like a dove and lighting on him. And a voice from heaven said, 'This is my Son, whom I love; with him I am well pleased'" (Matthew 3:16,17). Jesus was baptized. The Spirit descended. The Father spoke from heaven, acknowledging his Son. God is one, but three persons were present and participating.

The Son speaks of the Father and the Holy Spirit in John 14:26: "But the Counselor, the Holy Spirit, whom the Father will send in my name, will teach you all things and will remind you of everything I have said to you." Again in John 15:26, he says, "When the Counselor comes, whom I will send to you from the Father, the Spirit of truth who goes out from the Father, he will testify about me." Spirit, Son, Father—all three persons.

The apostle Peter addresses his first letter to God's elect, "who have been chosen according to the foreknowledge of God the Father, through the sanctifying work of the Spirit, for obedience to Jesus Christ and sprinkling by his blood" (1 Peter 1:2). These are only a few of the passages in the New Testament making specific mention of all three divine persons.

The unity of the three persons is such that no one can know the Father without the Son. Jesus says, "All things have been committed to me by my Father. No one knows the Son except the Father, and no one knows the Father except the Son and those to whom the Son chooses to reveal him" (Matthew 11:27).

The reverse is also true. After Simon Peter made his great confession as to who Jesus is, "Jesus replied, 'Blessed are you, Simon son of Jonah, for this was not revealed to you by man, but by my Father in heaven'" (Matthew 16:17). Likewise, we could not confess our Savior without the work of the Holy Spirit: "No one can say, 'Jesus is Lord,' except by the Holy Spirit" (1 Corinthians 12:3). Physically dead people cannot make decisions as to their physical welfare. Likewise, spiritually dead people cannot make decisions as to their spiritual welfare. Faith is a gift from God, not an achievement of man.

The Trinity in the Old Testament

The doctrine of the Trinity is not taught as explicitly and abundantly in the Old Testament as in the New. Nevertheless, we can see more than a few hints of it in the Old Testament. The Old Testament provided words used by the New Testament writers to express the truths concerning the Trinity: Father, Son, Spirit, Word, Wisdom. And as we shall see, the Old Testament does explicitly mention the three persons of the Godhead.

There is no question that Moses believed, "The LORD is one" (Deuteronomy 6:4). Yet, he quotes God as using plural forms to express himself. We notice the plural forms in Genesis 1:26, for example: "Then God said, 'Let *us* make man in our image, in *our* likeness, and let them rule over the fish of the sea and the birds of the air, over the livestock, over all the earth, and over all the creatures that move along the ground.'" The very next verse, however, refers to God with singular pronouns and singular Hebrew verb forms: "So *God created* man in *his* own image, in the image of God *he* created him; male and female *he* created them" (Genesis 1:27). Although God is three persons, God is one being. Long before the New Testament was written, Moses used language that makes it clear (at least to readers of the New Testament) that all three persons of the Trinity were active in creation. In Genesis 3:22, after the disobedience of Adam and Eve, God spoke with sad irony: "The man has now become like one of *us*, knowing good and evil. He must not be allowed to reach out his hand and take also from the tree of life and eat, and live forever." Moses, the great teacher of monotheism, quotes God using the plural again, as he also does in the story of the Tower of Babel. When the descendants of those who survived the flood decided to glorify themselves instead of God, God said, "Come, let *us* go down and confuse their language so they will not understand each other" (Genesis 11:7). Likewise, the prophet Isaiah reports: "Then I heard the voice of *the Lord* saying, 'Whom shall *I* send? And who will go for *us*?'" (Isaiah 6:8). Note the combination of plural and singular references, "I" and "us."

The threefold pronouncement of the Lord's name in the Aaronic blessing (Numbers 6:24-27) is paraphrased by Paul in the apostolic blessing of 2 Corinthians 13:14, which is unmistakably trinitarian: "May the grace of the Lord Jesus Christ, and the love of God, and the fellowship of the Holy Spirit be with you all." For New Testament believers, there is at least a suggestion of the Trinity in the threefold "holy" of Isaiah 6:3:

> And they were calling to one another:
>
> "Holy, holy, holy is the LORD Almighty;
>   the whole earth is full of his glory."

A verse from this same chapter (Isaiah 6:10) is quoted in John 12:40:

> "He has blinded their eyes
>   and deadened their hearts,

> so they can neither see with their eyes,
>   nor understand with their hearts,
>   nor turn—and I would heal them."

Then the evangelist John, with reference to Isaiah 6:10 and referring back to the vision of Isaiah 6:1-4, writes, "Isaiah said this because he saw Jesus' glory and spoke about him" (John 12:41).

Also quoting Isaiah 6:10, the apostle Paul said to the leaders of the Jews in Rome:

> The *Holy Spirit* spoke the truth to your forefathers when he said through Isaiah the prophet:

> "Go to this people and say,
> 'You will be ever hearing but never understanding;
>   you will be ever seeing but never perceiving.'
> For this people's heart has become calloused;
>   they hardly hear with their ears,
>   and they have closed their eyes.
> Otherwise they might see with their eyes,
>   hear with their ears,
>   understand with their hearts
> and turn, and I would heal them" (Acts 28:25-27).

These uses of Isaiah 6 in the New Testament leave no question that the angels who sang "Holy, holy, holy" were praising the Holy Trinity.

Old Testament passages that mention all three persons

There are also several passages in Isaiah in which the prophet actually mentions all three persons of the Trinity. In Isaiah 11:1,2, the prophet speaks of the Messiah as the shoot and Branch from the stump of Jesse. He speaks of the Spirit. He speaks of the Lord himself:

A shoot will come up from the stump of Jesse;
  from his roots a Branch will bear fruit.
The Spirit of the LORD will rest on him—
    the Spirit of wisdom and of understanding,
    the Spirit of counsel and of power,
    the Spirit of knowledge and of the fear of the LORD.

Isaiah quotes the Lord directly again in 42:1:

"Here is my servant, whom I uphold,
    my chosen one in whom I delight;
I will put my Spirit on him
    and he will bring justice to the nations."

The Lord speaks, he speaks of his servant (the Messiah), and he promises to endow his servant with his Spirit. Thus, all three persons of the Trinity are mentioned.

In Isaiah 48:16, the Messiah is speaking:

Come near me and listen to this:

"From the first announcement I have not spoken
      in secret;
    at the time it happens, I am there."
And now the Sovereign LORD has sent me,
    with his Spirit.

"I" (Messiah), "the Sovereign LORD," "his Spirit"—three persons.

In Isaiah 61:1, all three persons are clearly mentioned and distinguished from one another:

The Spirit of the Sovereign LORD is on me,
    because the LORD has anointed me
    to preach good news to the poor.
He has sent me to bind up the brokenhearted,
    to proclaim freedom for the captives
    and release from darkness for the prisoners.

In these several quotations, we have seen Isaiah, who
like Moses believed that there is only one God, repeatedly
quoting one or another of the persons of the Godhead as
that person addresses or refers to the other two. This is
amazing, and it certainly helps account for the fact that
the true Israelites who wrote the New Testament could
believe that Jesus is God and identify the Holy Spirit as a
third divine person. In fact, when Jesus called God his
Father, the Jews did not object to him saying that God has
a Son: "Jesus said to them, 'My Father is always at his work
to this very day, and I, too, am working.' For this reason
the Jews tried all the harder to kill him; not only was he
breaking the Sabbath, but he was even calling God his
own Father, making himself equal with God" (John
5:17,18). Notice that they did not deny that God has a
Son. Notice that what they objected to was that *Jesus*
claimed to be the Son of God. Notice too that, in their
minds, the Son of God is "equal with God."

Old Testament quoted in the book of Hebrews

The author of the epistle to the Hebrews cites a series of
Old Testament passages in chapter 1 to prove that Christ
is true God. In Hebrews 1:5, he quotes from Psalm 2:7 and
2 Samuel 7:14:

> For to which of the angels did God ever say,
>
> "You are my Son;
> > today I have become your Father"?
>
> Or again,
> "I will be his Father,
> > and he will be my Son"?

Paul quotes the psalm verse (2:7) in Acts 13:32,33 in
order to show that Jesus' resurrection proves he is the Son

of God: "We tell you the good news: What God promised our fathers he has fulfilled for us, their children, by raising up Jesus. As it is written in the second Psalm: 'You are my Son; today I have become your Father.'" The words in 2 Samuel 7:14, "I will be his father, and he will be my son," applied originally to Solomon, but they had a deeper meaning. They prophesied concerning King David's greater son, the Son of God, whose kingdom is eternal.

At Hebrews 1:6, the author quotes Psalm 97:7: "And again, when God brings his firstborn into the world, he says, 'Let all God's angels worship him.'" God wants Christ, his "firstborn" (acknowledged as first in rank and authority), to be worshiped by all the angels. Now, the angels are God's highest creatures. For them to *worship* Christ is to bow before someone greater and higher than themselves, their Creator. Incidentally, the inspired author here used the Greek translation of the Hebrew Old Testament. The psalmist says in Hebrew, "Worship him, all you *gods*," referring to the idols of the heathen. The Holy Spirit interprets his own book by inspiring the author of Hebrews to write "Let all God's *angels* worship him." The living angels, God's messengers, are higher than the dead gods of the nations are. These angels are to bow down in acknowledgment that Christ is higher than all other creatures.

In Hebrews 1:7-9, we read:

In speaking of the angels he says,

"He makes his angels winds,
    his servants flames of fire."

But about the Son he says,

"Your throne, O God, will last for ever and ever,
    and righteousness will be the scepter of
        your kingdom.

> You have loved righteousness and hated wickedness;
>   therefore God, your God, has set you above your
>   companions
>   by anointing you with the oil of joy."

The author first quotes Psalm 104:4 to acknowledge the excellence of the angels. Then he quotes Psalm 45:6,7 to show Christ's superiority over the angels and all creatures. Did we say *Christ's*? Yes. Who is the Anointed One, anointed "with the oil of joy"? The Hebrew word *Messiah* means "Anointed." In Greek it is "Christ." The psalmist is addressing the Messiah, Christ, and he addresses him as "God." Messiah's throne is eternal, he will rule justly, and so his God (the Lord God of Israel) has set him above all his companions, making him superior to all.

Psalm 102:25-27 reads:

> In the beginning you laid the foundations of the earth,
>   and the heavens are the work of your hands.
> They will perish, but you remain;
>   they will all wear out like a garment.
> Like clothing you will change them
>   and they will be discarded.
> But you remain the same,
>   and your years will never end.

The author of Hebrews quotes this psalm and applies the words to Jesus Christ, the Son of God (Hebrews 1:10-12). In the beginning of creation, before there was anything or anyone except God, the Son was there, participating in the work of creating the universe. Through the ages the universe has been wearing out and finally will be discarded and replaced. The Son, however, remains the same. His years will never end. He is the eternal God.

Psalm 110:1 reads:

> The LORD says to my Lord:
> "Sit at my right hand
> until I make your enemies
>   a footstool for your feet.

Hebrews 1:13 asks: "To which of the angels did God ever say, 'Sit at my right hand until I make your enemies a footstool for your feet'?" Again, the Messiah is superior to all creatures, including the angels. The position of supreme authority and power, God's right hand, is reserved for him. He has conquered all his enemies and will demonstrate it by placing his foot on their necks. In Matthew 22:41-45, Jesus quoted this same psalm verse to prove to the Pharisees that the Messiah is not only David's son but also David's Lord:

> While the Pharisees were gathered together, Jesus asked them, "What do you think about the Christ? Whose son is he?"
>
> "The son of David," they replied.
>
> He said to them, "How is it then that David, speaking by the Spirit, calls him 'Lord'? For he says,
>
>> "'The Lord said to my Lord:
>>   "Sit at my right hand
>> until I put your enemies
>>   under your feet."'
>
> If then David calls him 'Lord,' how can he be his son?"

(Compare Mark 12:35-37; Luke 20:41-44.)

Certainly the Jews who believed that Jesus is the Messiah were able to find all three persons of the Godhead, and especially Christ, in the Old Testament.

7

The Trinity: One God

We speak of the *unity* of God in order to say that God is one essential being, that there is no other God and we must not think of him as divided into parts.

By *being* (essence, substance) we mean that very thing in God by which he is God—separate from all else. God's creatures appear in multitudes. There are billions of people, innumerable dogs, and countless insects. But there is only one God. He is unique, unduplicated, in a class by himself. In a world of false gods, the true God taught his people to confess, "Hear, O Israel: The LORD our God, the LORD is one. Love the LORD your God with all your heart and with all your soul and with all your strength" (Deuteronomy 6:4,5). Jesus called this the most important commandment

(Mark 12:29). In the New Testament, the apostle Paul writes, "So then, about eating food sacrificed to idols: We know that an idol is nothing at all in the world and that there is no God but one" (1 Corinthians 8:4).

There is no other God

Through his prophet Isaiah, God proclaimed:

"You are my witnesses," declares the LORD,
   "and my servant whom I have chosen,
so that you may know and believe me
   and understand that I am he.
Before me no god was formed,
   nor will there be one after me." (Isaiah 43:10).

Also:

"I am the LORD, and there is no other;
   apart from me there is no God.
I will strengthen you,
   though you have not acknowledged me"
      (Isaiah 45:5).

There is not a genus that is called god, of which the Maker and Preserver of all things is one species. God is absolutely unique, without any duplicate or peer. "Before me [there was] no god." "Apart from me there is no God."

God is not divided

We must not think of God as divided into parts. In the realm of God's creatures, three individual human beings cannot properly be called one man. The men are three separate beings, not just one. Although God is Father, Son, and Holy Spirit, God is one being, not three. The Father, the Son, or the Holy Spirit would be less than God if one of them were separated from the other two persons in any way. The Bible *distinguishes* among the three, but does not *separate* them. It does not speak of three parts of God or of a threefold God. God is one. God is triune, three in one; not triplex, made up of three parts.

Analogies

Through the centuries many comparisons and illustrations from nature have been used to represent or picture the doctrine of the Trinity. None of them can explain the mystery. None of them can prove that God is triune or even that he could be triune. Not one fully illustrates the teaching of the Scriptures on the subject. Believers might find some help for understanding the Trinity in some of them, but none of them will satisfy or convert the unbeliever. Some analogies could or actually do misrepresent the doctrine. It is important to remember that the doctrine of the Trinity was not drawn from and is not based on groupings of three in other religions or on triads or triplexes in nature. The teaching of the Three-in-One comes from Holy Scripture alone. The various analogies were devised later.

Because they are popular even though not entirely helpful, a few examples of such analogies are in place. The Trinity has been compared to the sun, which has fire, light, and heat. These attributes do not really correspond to what the Scripture says about Father, Son, and Holy Spirit—although they can illustrate (not prove) that the Father is not diminished by sharing his divinity with the Son and Spirit. Yet, the persons of the Trinity are not attributes of God in the way fire, light, and heat are attributes of the sun. Rather, each person is himself God, while flame, light, and heat are not in themselves the sun.

The same must be said about the analogy of body, soul, and spirit in a human being. None of the three components is in and of itself a human being. But each person of the Trinity is himself God. Likewise consider the analogy of human psychology suggested by Augustine—understanding, will, and memory. None of these properties by itself constitutes a human being, while each person of the Trinity is in himself truly God. Analogies in general tend to be more fanciful than helpful and could actually lead to serious confusion in our thinking about God.

A useful but limited symbol of the Trinity is the equilateral triangle. That the three sides are equal to one another reminds us of the equality of persons. The three individual sides remind us that the three persons are distinct from one another. Each angle includes the entire area of the triangle, illustrating the fact that each person of the Trinity has in him the entire divine being. Finally, each angle permeates the other two, an illustration of the *perichoresis* (pair-ee-KOR-ee-zis) or interpenetration of each person by the other two. This symbol pictures some of what the Bible teaches, but none of this explains the mystery or proves the doctrine. The same must be said of the symbol of three interlocking circles, which also symbolizes the eternity of each person.

The shamrock and the fleur-de-lis have long been used as illustrations of the Trinity. Three separate leaves or blooms in combination do form one clover or lily. What the three form, however, is a fourth thing. Father, Son, and Holy Spirit are each God, and they do not combine to form a fourth entity or being.

Someone has said that the doctrine of the Trinity is "supremely unpicturable." The greatest theologians have failed to "draw" it. We must simply try to repeat after God what he says in the Bible, knowing that in his unity of being and in his trinity of persons he is beyond our ability to comprehend. On the other hand, we do not look down on those who have suggested analogies and pictures in the attempt to treat a very difficult subject.

The triune God's activity
In and toward the created world: undivided

God is one being. There are not three gods but one. Since he is one in being, God has only one will and one set of divine attributes. Therefore, he is also one and undivided in his actions. The church's teachers have expressed it in this way: "God's works toward what is outside of himself are undivided." Even when only one person of the Trinity is mentioned in Scripture, it is God who acts, and therefore the other persons are also involved.

True, the history of God's dealing with his creation—especially with the human race—speaks of the particular work of each person of the Trinity. The particular work of the Father is creation, of the Son, redemption, and of the Holy Spirit, sanctification. These distinctions are made in the creeds and acknowledged in the church's worship. Yet, the other persons are likewise involved. The work of God is cooperative work, not divided among but shared by the three persons. Jesus said to his disciples, "My Father is always at his work to this very day, and I, too, am working. For just as the Father raises the dead and gives them life, even so the Son gives life to whom he is pleased to give it" (John 5:17,21).

The Son was involved in the work of creation, as was pointed out in chapter 3. John 1:3 says concerning the second person: "Through him all things were made; without him nothing was made that has been made." Paul wrote concerning the Son: "For by him all things were created: things in heaven and on earth, visible and invisible, whether thrones or powers or rulers or authorities; all things were created by him and for him" (Colossians 1:16). Our Redeemer is also the Creator of all that is and Lord of the universe. The author of Hebrews writes: "In these last days he [God] has spoken to us by his Son, whom he appointed heir of all things, and through whom he made the universe. The Son is the radiance of God's glory and the exact representation of his being, sustaining all things by his powerful word. After he had provided purification for sins, he sat down at the right hand of the Majesty in heaven" (Hebrews 1:2,3). Not only was the Son involved in creation, he is also involved in the preservation of the universe.

Like the Father and the Son, the Holy Spirit was also involved in the creation of the universe, and he continues to create new life today, as Elihu confessed: "The Spirit of God has made me; the breath of the Almighty gives me life" (Job 33:4). In Psalm 104:30, the Father and the Holy Spirit are mentioned together in the continuing work of creation: "When you send your Spirit, they are created, and you renew the face of the earth."

Jesus the Redeemer acknowledges the presence and work of the Spirit when he speaks of his own particular work:

"The Spirit of the Lord is on me,
    because he has anointed me
    to preach good news to the poor.
He has sent me to proclaim freedom for the prisoners
    and recovery of sight for the blind,
    to release the oppressed,
        to proclaim the year of the Lord's favor."
(Luke 4:18)

Only the second person became truly human, but the Father sent him for our redemption (John 3:16; Galatians 4:4,5); and he was conceived through the agency of the Holy Spirit (Matthew 1:18).

Although sanctification is the particular work of the Holy Spirit, *Christ the Redeemer* has also acted to sanctify his church, that is, to make it holy: "Christ loved the church and gave himself up for her to make her holy, cleansing her by the washing with water through the word" (Ephesians 5:25,26). Jesus addressed the *Father* when he prayed: "Sanctify them by the truth; your word is truth" (John 17:17). Paul involves all three persons in the privilege and exercise of prayer, an important aspect of sanctified living: "For through him [Christ] we both [Jews and Gentiles] have access to the Father by one Spirit" (Ephesians 2:18). All three persons work to build us up into mature Christians: "And in him [Christ] you too are being built together to become a dwelling in which God lives by his Spirit" (Ephesians 2:22). Thus we see that all three persons are involved in calling, enlightening, and sanctifying believers—the "particular" work of the Holy Spirit. Jesus says in John 14:16: "I will ask the Father, and he will give you another Counselor to be with you forever." Again, notice all three persons.

Within himself: divided

The inner workings of the Godhead, unlike God's works toward the created world, are divided. Toward the world which they have created and redeemed, the persons of the Trinity work together, undivided. But their "work," or actions and relationships, toward one another are not the same, and so we say they are divided. Scripture says much that is explicit and plain about the separate identity and particular work "toward the outside" of each of the three persons in the one Godhead. Much of what we say about the inner life, or work within himself, of the triune God we say more by inference than on the basis of direct Bible references.

God's actions "to the inside" had no beginning and will have no end. They are eternal and therefore continuous and uninterrupted. These actions express and reveal the relationships among the three. Actively, the Father generates (begets) the Son. Passively, the Son is generated (begotten), because he is the Son and the Father is the Father. The Son and the Holy Spirit do not generate or beget. The Father and the Son spirate (breathe) the Spirit and thus he proceeds from them. The Spirit does not breathe out either the Father or the Son. Thus we say again that their inward works are divided.

The Spirit proceeds (is breathed out) from both Father and Son because, as explained in chapter 4, he is the Spirit of *both* Father *and* Son. Matthew 10:20 says that he is the Spirit of the Father: "It will not be you speaking, but the Spirit of your Father speaking through you." Galatians 4:6 says that he is the Spirit of the Son: "Because you are sons, God sent the Spirit of his Son into our hearts, the Spirit who calls out, 'Abba, Father.'"

The Father is neither generated (begotten) nor breathed. He does not "proceed" from either of the other persons. Again, this is why we say that the inward works of the Trinity are divided.

The three persons exist and have eternally existed in union with one another, in one being. No one of the three has ever existed apart from the others. The relationship of each person to the others is one of love and mutual glorification. There is one consciousness, one will, one set of attributes. The relationship of each person of the God-head to the others is not like that of species to genus or of attribute to essence. As they are coeternal, so they are coequal in majesty. There is nothing of the superior or the subordinate in their eternal relationship, although in time—in the work of redeeming the world—there was a temporary subordination of the Son to the Father.

This inner life, these inner workings of the Trinity in unity are beyond our comprehension. What we have said in this section about the inner workings and relationship is simply a way of expressing what every Christian knows. Every Christian knows that the Son is the Father's one and only Son from eternity to eternity and the Holy Spirit is the Spirit of the Father and of the Son from eternity to eternity.

8

Some Ancient Errors and Their Modern Counterparts

Almost three thousand years ago, King Solomon wrote:

> What has been will be again,
>> what has been done will be done again;
>> there is nothing new under the sun. (Ecclesiastes 1:9)

Many of the errors concerning Christ and the Trinity that confronted the church in the earliest centuries of its existence have reappeared in later centuries under new names and wearing new faces. This age is certainly not exempt. We can guard against repeating the errors of the past if we are willing to learn from those who first dealt with them. They found the appropriate language and formulations to correct them and to express the biblical truth concerning the Holy Trinity.

Already late in the first century, the apostle John, in his first epistle, warned against men who were teaching falsely regarding Christ's incarnation, denying that the eternal divine Word did indeed become flesh. John wrote:

> Dear friends, do not believe every spirit, but test the spirits to see whether they are from God, because many false prophets have gone out into the world. This is how you can recognize the Spirit of God: Every spirit that acknowledges that Jesus Christ has come in the flesh is from God, but every spirit that does not acknowledge Jesus is not from God. This is the spirit of the antichrist, which you have heard is coming and even now is already in the world (1 John 4:1-3).

Denials of Christ's true divinity

The Ebionites (EH-be-un-ites), Hebrew for "the poor," were Jews who believed that Jesus was the Messiah. However, they denied his virgin birth and did not believe in his divinity. They regarded the apostle Paul as a traitor to the true faith, one who had perverted the gospel.

The Elkesaites (El-KEY-sah-ites) were an offshoot of the Ebionites, founded by Elkesai (EL-keh-sigh) around the year 100. Elkesai claimed that he had received a book from heaven, the true teaching about Jesus. He taught that Jesus was a prophet like Moses, come to preach the truth and to gather the righteous. Both of these groups, as we see, claimed to be Christian and yet denied a basic truth of the Christian gospel: Jesus Christ is God come in the flesh.

The cult of Elkesai survived in Arabia and had some influence on Muhammad (ca. 570–632), the founder of Islam. Much that Islam's Koran says about Jesus agrees with Elkesai's teaching. Jesus, according to the Koran, was a virgin-born prophet, he ascended into heaven, and he will return. He is not, however, God's incarnate Son. The Koran says: "The Christians say: The Messiah is the son of Allah. That is their saying with their mouths. They imitate the saying of those who disbelieved of old. Allah (himself) fighteth against them. How perverse are they!"[17] The Koran also says, "Jesus, son of Mary, was only a messenger of Allah and His Word which he conveyed unto Mary, and a spirit from Him. So believe in God and His messengers, and say not, 'Three.'"[18] A Jordanian guide once put it more briefly and mildly: "We do not believe God has a family."

Docetism—denial of Christ's true humanity

As mentioned previously, an early false teaching about Christ was Docetism (DOE-seat-izm). This doctrine wanted to honor Jesus as true God, but it deprived him of his true humanity. Taking the view that it was improper and impossible for almighty God to be born, suffer, and die, Docetists taught that the Son of God only *seemed* (Latin *docet*, DOE-ket) to be human. In their view he was actually a kind of phantom, or a projection of the divine, not really sharing in our humanity. In the second century, Marcion (MAR-see-un) actually deleted Jesus' words in Luke 24:39 in the interest of his docetic system: "Look at my hands and my feet. It is I myself! Touch me and see; a ghost does not have flesh and bones, as you see I have." Marcion's purpose was to deny that Christ was a truly physical and material being, especially after he was glorified. Marcion was one of many teachers who were strongly influenced by the Gnostics (NAHS-ticks), a group about whom we shall hear more.

The apostolic fathers

The apostolic fathers were men who knew or could have known one or more of Jesus' apostles personally. Although some of their works may have been written earlier, the time of their activity is generally thought to be from the late 90s to about early 150. They all insisted that there is only one God. They all affirmed that Christ is divine and that he came to this earth as Jesus. They believed that Christ existed before the creation and many spoke of his work in the creation of all things. Several of them used the expression "Father, Son, and Holy Spirit." None of them had much to say about the Holy Spirit, in part because his work was evident in the life of the church and in part because heretics were not denying or attacking his person and work as they were already doing in the case of the Father and the Son. Unfortunately, while all of these apostolic fathers were very careful not to speak of Christ as "created," each of them in one way or another spoke of the Son as subordinate to the Father and not really eternal.

Apologists

The Apologists, a group of mostly second-century Christian writers, were defenders, or "explainers," of the faith. Earnest Christians and learned men, they tried to explain the relationship of Christ and the Father, especially to non-Christians. They did not have the advantage we have in being able to build on the efforts of great men of the past. In their efforts they sometimes made statements that were inadequate, unclear, or even in error. For example, they theorized that the Logos (the Word) was not eternal, but came into existence before the creation, so that he could participate in the creating work. Especially, they tended to subordinate both the Son and the Holy Spirit to the Father.

Gnosticism

One of the greatest threats to the church in the age after the apostles—a much greater threat than government persecution—was Gnosticism (NAHS-ti-sizm). Gnosticism did not originate in the church, but it did find adherents there. Gnostics claimed to have knowledge that ordinary people lacked. Gnosticism was a pseudoscience, much as evolutionism is today. There were a variety of gnostic systems, but all tended to have certain things in common.

Among Christians who were caught up in this false belief system, knowledge was considered to be more desirable than faith. Those who had special knowledge revealed to them were supposed to be superior to other Christians. Gnostics gave speculative answers to questions that the Bible neither asks nor answers. Or, they were not satisfied with the Bible's answers. For example, they asked the very "modern" question: "If God is good and God is almighty, why does he permit evil in the world?" The Gnostics' answer was that the Creator God of the Old Testament was inept, a blind force that could not work intelligently or effectively. This ineptitude, they taught, resulted in the imperfection of the material world and, thus, resulted in sin. They regarded creation as a fall or a "devolution" from the spiritual world to the material, from the divine to the corrupt. Salvation they thought of as an evolution or a regeneration, in which the spirit is delivered from the prison of the body through knowledge (Greek *gnosis*, NO-zis). Freed from the material and the physical, the spirit can finally be caught up into the "fullness of deity." Although they used biblical vocabulary, they explained away the literal words of Scripture and assigned "spiritual" (allegorical) meanings to them. They did not hesitate to add myths to the biblical accounts in order to bolster their teachings.

There do not seem to have been fully developed gnostic *systems* at the time the New Testament was written. Gnostic *ideas*, however, were already troubling some Christian believers. Paul wrote to the Christians at Colosse: "See to it that no one takes you captive through hollow and deceptive philosophy, which depends on human tradition and the basic principles of this world rather than on Christ. For in Christ all the fullness of the Deity lives in bodily form" (Colossians 2:8,9). *Basic principles* and *fullness* were expressions that Gnostics frequently used. Paul seemed to be urging his readers to steer clear of gnostic ideas about the "fullness of the Deity" and focus on Christ, in whom the fullness of the Deity lives. Even the expression *in bodily form* might be aimed at the gnostic idea that the body is inherently evil.

To Timothy, Paul wrote: "Guard what has been entrusted to your care. Turn away from godless chatter and the opposing ideas of what is falsely called knowledge, which some have professed and in so doing have wandered from the faith" (1 Timothy 6:20,21). The expression *falsely called knowledge* could also be translated "Gnosis falsely named." The King James Version translates it "science falsely so called." Paul's words of warning certainly apply today!

The most damaging error of the Gnostics was to deny the fundamental Christian truth that the "Word became flesh" (John 1:14), that in Christ God did really become fully human. In their view, since flesh and blood are matter and matter is evil or a "mirage," the holy and divine

Son of God could not have assumed a truly human nature. In the gnostic systems that gave any divine honor to Christ, he was treated as a spirit being, who only seemed to be human (Docetism). Jesus was not "the heart and core of Bible lore," since in their view he was only one of several mediators through whom God has given knowledge to the human race. There was not much interest in the Jesus of the four gospels.

Modern examples of Gnosticism

Christian Science is a modern example of Gnosticism. According to the teaching of Mary Baker Eddy, the virgin mother conceived an idea of God and gave it the name Jesus. Mary's child was the offspring of her self-conscious communion with the divine. Her child is not God, since God is an impersonal principle or infinite mind. Jesus is not Christ, because Christ is simply the divine ideal. "Science," incidentally, is one way in which to translate the Greek word *gnosis* (knowledge).

Christian Science has a "twin sister," the Unity School of Christianity. In this system, a distinction is made between the man Jesus and the Christ. The Christ is simply God's thought of what man ought to be. Jesus is the outer man, and Christ is the spiritual identity. The man Jesus was not God incarnate but a reincarnation of King David. Jesus demonstrated the Christ in his life and thus manifested that he was truly *a* (not *the*) son of God. The Theosophical Society is another example of a group that teaches a gnostic Christ.

The Latter-day Saints (Mormons) list the Bible first among their standard works, but they teach a gnostic Christ on the basis of their other standard works and the continuing revelations of their presidents.

The Christ of the Jehovah's Witnesses was created as the Archangel Michael. He was the brother of the angel who sinned, Satan. The man Jesus was a perfect human being but nothing more. He did not rise bodily from the dead. Since his body was missing from the tomb it may have dissolved in gases, or it may have been removed supernaturally and preserved as a grand memorial. The spirit of Jesus rose as a divine being (Michael again) and returned as king of the earth in 1914. He did not and will not return visibly because he has no body.

Monarchianism

Jews sometimes accused the early Christians of believing in more than one God because they confessed "Jesus is Lord." Gentile philosophers also asked why Christians condemned the heathen for having many gods when the Christians themselves worshiped Father, Son, and Holy Spirit. Tertullian (d. ca. 222), theologian at Carthage in North Africa, spoke in this way of the problem ordinary Christians can have with the doctrine of the Trinity: "The simple, indeed, (I will not call them unwise and unlearned,) who always constitute the majority of believers, are startled at the dispensation (of the Three in One), on the ground that their very rule of faith withdraws them from the world's plurality of gods to the one only true God."[19] The Lord our God is One? How can three persons be worshiped as one God?

Some teachers in the third century put so much emphasis on the unity or oneness of God that they were called Monarchians (mon-ARK-ee-ans). The Greek roots of this word express the concept of "one being" or "one ruler." Monarchianism took two forms, the modal and the dynamist.

Modal Monarchianism

One incorrect solution to the difficulty of the Three-in-One teaching is to say that Father, Son, and Spirit are not three distinct persons. The modal Monarchians denied the individual personalities of Father, Son, and Holy Spirit. Rather, they said, each is a mode of God's activity—now creating, now redeeming, now sanctifying. Some theologians, in an attempt to be helpful, even spoke of God's three masks or roles (Latin *personae*, per-SO-ni, from which the word *persons* comes). In the Monarchian thinking, Father, Son, and Holy Spirit are one and equal but not distinct from one another. It was actually possible for some of them to say, "The Father was crucified for us." They were called Patripassianists, those who teach that the Father (*Patri-*) suffered (*passianists*). The best known of the modalists was Sabellius, who was condemned by a gathering of bishops that met in 268 and 269 at Antioch in Syria.

Jesus' words in Matthew 28:19, from which our formula for Baptism is taken, provide one testimony that there are three distinct persons, not three masks or modes. The 17th-century Lutheran theologian John Gerhard put it thus: "The Father receives the baptized person as his child, the Son as his brother, the Holy Spirit as his temple and habitation."[20]

Oneness Pentecostalism (mentioned in chapter 3) is a modern example of modalism. Unlike Mormons and Jehovah's Witnesses, Oneness Pentecostalists teach that Jesus is truly God. But then they say that he is the *only* person in the Godhead. The followers of Emanuel Swedenborg (d. 1772), who reject the scriptural doctrine of the Trinity, teach that the trinity of "love, wisdom, and activity" are aspects of one person.

Dynamic Monarchianism

The same gathering of bishops that condemned Sabellius at Antioch during the synod of 268–269 also condemned Paul of Samosata (Sah-MOE-sah-tah) for his "dynamism." Said the Synod of Antioch: "He [Paul] will not confess with us that the Son of God descended from heaven."[21] Dynamism says that at some point in time, perhaps at his conception or his baptism, Christ received divine power to do his divine works. Thus, he was not the eternal God become flesh. Rather, said Paul, an impersonal power from God resided in him. Paul of Samosata is remembered especially for forbidding the congregation at Antioch to offer prayers and hymns to Jesus as God. He insisted that Christ is not "from above" but "from below"—a mere human being imbued with God's power. Like the modalist Sabellius, Paul thought his teaching safeguarded the oneness of God.

A form of dynamism, today more often called Adoptionism, appears in some Protestant churches when Jesus is mistakenly presented as a perfect man whom God has exalted to divine status by adopting him as his Son. The Lutheran church's Formula of Concord condemns the error of some of the Anabaptists, "that Christ is not true God but that he only has more gifts of the Holy Spirit than any other holy person."[22]

Subordinationism

Unfortunately, some of those who made good contributions to the development of sound teaching on the Trinity also spoke of the Son as subordinate to the Father. The apologist Justin Martyr, executed by the Roman government in about 165, taught that the Son is the Father's servant, dependent on him and not having all the divine attributes or characteristics.

While Origen insisted that the Son is truly God from eternity, he regarded the Son (and the Holy Spirit) as in some way secondary and subordinate to the Father. He did not simply mean that Jesus subordinated himself to his Father in carrying out his earthly ministry. He meant that the Son is subordinate to the Father in the Godhead, not an ordinary creature but not God in the strictest and most absolute sense either. At one point he even suggested that Father and Son are "two gods," although one in power.

Jesus *did* subordinate himself to the Father in carrying out his earthly ministry. "The Father is greater than I," Jesus said (John 14:28). Not making all his divine characteristics evident, not asserting all his divine authority, and not exercising all his divine power according to his human nature, he could say, "The world must learn that I love the Father and that I do exactly what my Father has commanded me" (John 14:31). The apostle Paul, in Philippians, tells us that Christ Jesus humbled himself and became obedient. By that very action, Jesus shows that he is by nature the Son of God, equal with God. It means that he is not *essentially* subordinate. "Being in very nature God, [he] did not consider equality with God something to be grasped, but made himself nothing, taking the very nature of a servant, being made in human likeness. And being found in appearance as a man, he humbled himself and became obedient to death—even death on a cross!" (Philippians 2:6-8). He could not cease to be what he eternally has been. His deity could not be taken away from him. When he came to redeem the world of sinners, however, he willingly set aside the full display of his divine majesty and the full use of his divine powers as the

God-man. Jesus did not use for his own advantage in time what has been his by right from eternity.

"For you know the grace of our Lord Jesus Christ, that though he was rich, yet for your sakes he became poor, so that you through his poverty might become rich" (2 Corinthians 8:9). As the Son of God from eternity, he is the Lord of the universe, infinitely rich. There was, there is, nothing that does not belong to him. He became poor for our sakes by temporarily setting aside the full and continuous use of his divine powers and abilities.

Let us not lose sight of what Jesus accomplished by assuming our poverty in obedience to the Father. "Just as the result of one trespass was condemnation for all men, so also the result of one act of righteousness was justification that brings life for all men. For just as through the disobedience of the one man the many were made sinners, so also through the obedience of the one man the many will be made righteous" (Romans 5:18,19). Through Jesus' humble obedience "the many will be made righteous." *Many* does not mean "some." It means "all." The same *many* who were made sinners in Adam's trespass are declared righteous on the basis of Christ's submissive obedience, his "one act of righteousness."

9

Arianism

Arius

Arius (AIR-ee-us) was a presbyter (priest) in Alexandria, Egypt, who accused his bishop of being a Sabellian—a modal Monarchian. Specifically, he objected to his bishop's use of the Greek word *homoousios* (hum-uh-OOZ-ee-us) to express the relationship that exists between the Father and the Son. The word means "of the same essence (being)." The problem with the word *homoousios*, a problem recognized by others as well as Arius, was that Sabellius had used the word to teach that Father, Son, and Holy Spirit are simply three different modes, or manifestations, of God, rather than three distinct persons. However, Arius' problem with his bishop is not the reason we remember him. We mention it here because we shall see that the word *homoousios* became a very useful word, even while it remained a troublesome word for some.

In 320, the Synod of Alexandria declared Arius a heretic, deposed him from office, and excommunicated him. The real reason we remember Arius is that he denied that the Son of God is God from eternity and that Jesus Christ is the eternal Son of God incarnate. Arius studied the New Testament, the writings of Christian teachers of the second century (the Apologists), and especially Origen, and came to the correct conclusion that Christ is the Son of God. But Arius also came to the mistaken conclusion that the Son is a lesser god, inferior and subordinate to the Father, and not eternal.

What did Arius actually teach concerning the second person of the Trinity? He said that the Son of God is God's highest creature, made out of nothing before the creation of the world, divine but not eternal. "There was once when he was not," said Arius. He could not say, "There was *a time* when he was not," because he taught that Christ was created in eternity—before time began. He wrote to a friend: "Before he was begotten or created or ordained or founded, he was not." Arius also said, "He was made out of nothing."[23] God, according to Arius, created the Son to be his agent in creating the world. Christ is a sort of second God. Since the true God is above and beyond the world, he could not become incarnate. Since God cannot suffer, he who died on the cross cannot be the eternal God.

Part of Arius' problem was that he misunderstood the concept of *begotten* in reference to the relationship between Father and Son—an error not too difficult to understand. *Begotten* had been used by Origen and others (and is used in the Nicene Creed) to express the truth that the Son was *not made*, that he is not a creature. *Begotten* does not refer to an event but to a relationship. It says that the relationship of the second person to the first person is one of sonship. In speaking of human relationships, *begetting* implies an event in time and includes the fact that the one begotten is younger than the one who begets. When the term *only begotten* is applied to the second person of the Trinity, however, it does not signify an event in time. Rather, it signifies an eternal relationship, without beginning and without end. As Origen of Alexandria said, "Who that is capable of entertaining reverential thoughts or feelings regarding God, can suppose or believe that God the Father ever existed, even for a moment of time, without having generated this Wisdom [the Son]?"[24] To say it more simply and briefly: The Son is eternally the Son because the Father is eternally the Father.

Readers who are familiar with the King James Version of the Bible know that John 3:16 reads "only begotten Son." That reading expresses a correct theological truth regarding the relationship between Father and Son. It is, however, a mistranslation. The Greek word in question is *monogenes* (mah-no-gen-ACE), which means "unique, in a class by himself, one of a kind." The New International Version correctly translates "one and only."

The Council of Nicaea (325)

There were a few church leaders who agreed with Arius and protested his excommunication. Those who really understood the significance of what Arius was saying were a minority. Nevertheless, his teaching endangered the entire gospel teaching, and the controversy threatened to divide the church. Emperor Constantine thought that a united church was needed to help preserve the unity of the Roman Empire. On the advice of the Spanish bishop Hosius (or Osius) of Cordoba, he summoned all the bishops of the empire to a synod. This synod is remembered as the first ecumenical (universal) council, although only one bishop from the West was in attendance. It came to be regarded as ecumenical because all Christians everywhere finally accepted its great doctrinal decision.

In what is now Turkey, southeast of Constantinople (today Istanbul), in Nicaea (today Iznik), the bishops convened on May 20, 325. There were 318 of them, about one-sixth of the total number of bishops in the empire. The man who presided was not a bishop of the church, and not even a baptized Christian at the time. That was Constantine. The man whose name is especially remembered for his role in settling the controversy was not a bishop at the time either. That was Athanasius.

Deacon Athanasius of Alexandria was the trusted secretary of his bishop, and as his theological advisor, he indirectly influenced the outcome of the synod. Athanasius' concern was practical. He recognized that the question of whether Christ is truly God has to do with the salvation of the human race. He insisted, correctly, that only God can save. He also pointed out that for the Scriptures to call Jesus Christ God and for the liturgy to address him as God would be idolatry if he were not, in fact, true God. Athanasius said, "He became man that we might become divine."[25] He did not, of course, mean that we will become gods. Rather, because of the work of Christ, we will at last have perfect knowledge of God and become holy and immortal.

At the council (synod) the debate finally focused on two Greek words, almost identical in spelling but vastly different in meaning. Is Christ homoousios (hum-uh-OOZ-ee-us, the word Arius had objected to), of the *same* being as God the Father? Or, is Christ *homoiousios* (hum-oi-OOZ-ee-us), of *like* or *similar* being as the Father? In Athanasius' view, *homoousios* expresses the truth that Christ is in essence true God from eternity. God is not a courtesy title for the Son. God is who he *is*. That word and that truth prevailed at Nicaea, not only because Athanasius urged it but also, in no small way, because Emperor Constantine insisted on it. The synod (council) formulated a creed to express it. The little letter *i* was not allowed.

The Creed of Nicaea contains much that is familiar to people who know the Nicene Creed today, including the expression "of one being *(homoousios)* with the Father." The Third Article reads simply "And in the Holy Spirit," because up to that time there had been no serious controversy concerning the person and work of the Spirit. There was an appendix to the creed, condemning those who agreed with Arius or who held to other errors regarding the second person: "But those who say that there was when he was not, and before he was begotten he was not, and he was made out of things that were not; or those who say that the Son of God was from a different hypostasis (he-PUH-stah-zis) or *ousia* (oo-ZEE-ah) or a creature, or capable of change or alteration, these the Catholic Church anathematizes."[26]

Problems after the Council of Nicaea

Only Arius and one bishop refused to bow to the Emperor's authority and accept the creed. Another bishop, Eusebius of Nicomedia, was deposed and excommunicated even though he accepted the decision and the creed. In later years he turned Constantine against Athanasius. Athanasius was exiled a total of five times by Constantine and his successors. There were times when it seemed the whole world was against Athanasius and that only he was holding to the truth that is summarized in *homoousios*.

There were two problems with the choice of words in the Creed of Nicaea, problems that continued to plague the church for another 56 years. First, the word *homoousios* had been used by Sabellius to teach modalism, which denies that God is three distinct persons. For that reason, many theologians in the East, who actually agreed with Athanasius and rejected Arianism, found the word unsuitable. Second, *hypostasis* and *ousia* were used by Eastern theologians as synonyms, both to refer to God's being (essence, substance). Between 325 and 381, theologians gradually came to use the word *hypostasis*, in the sense of "person," to refer to each of the three persons of the Trinity. They reserved the word *ousia* to refer to God's being. Here they followed the lead of Western theologians, who had for some time distinguished between substance or essence (being) on the one hand and person (expressing the individuality of Father, Son, and Holy Spirit) on the other hand.

Under succeeding emperors and in a constantly changing religious climate, there were compromise creeds that avoided using the word *homoousios*, "the same as" the Father. Other creeds used expressions such as "in all things similar to the Father," "of another being than the Father," "like the Father," and even—in the case of Eunomius and his followers—"unlike the Father." Not only bishops and theologians occupied themselves with these issues. Some of the common people sang Arian jingles, while others argued in favor of Athanasius' teaching.

The church agrees upon terminology

In a meeting at Alexandria in 362, the aged Athanasius conferred with three Eastern theologians who are remembered as the Great Cappadocians because they came from the region in southeastern Asia Minor known as Cappadocia. Basil of Caesarea, Gregory of Nazianz, and Gregory of Nyssa were able to explain the problem that existed in the East regarding the use of *homoousios:* It had been the term Sabellius used to teach modalism. Athanasius was able to explain the sense in which he and the Western church were using it: to express the equality of the Father, Son, and Holy Spirit—not to deny that they are distinct from one another but to avoid surrendering the unity of God's being. The Cappadocians said that they had always believed in the equality of the three persons and the oneness of God, without using the word *homoousios* to express it.

At the end of their meeting, Athanasius and the Cappadocians agreed on a revised form of a creed called the Creed of Jerusalem. The Cappadocians worked to convince their fellow orthodox bishops and theologians that Athanasius and those who agreed with him were not modalists.

Recall that the words *hypostasis* and *ousia* had both been used in the sense of "being" at Nicaea. Now the Cappadocians and Athanasius (and others) agreed that *hypostasis* should be used to express the distinct identities of Father, Son, and Holy Spirit—their personhood. The word *ousia,* on the other hand, would be used for the one being that the three persons share. Other synods in other parts of the Roman Empire came to similar conclusions during the two decades that followed.

Full agreement among all the church's leaders was delayed when 35 Egyptian bishops, followers of Macedon, denied that the Holy Spirit is equal with the Father and the Son. They regarded *spirit* as simply referring to the spiritual gifts poured out on believers. The Macedonians earned for themselves the nickname Pneumatomachians (Noo-mat-oh-MAY-key-ans), "fighters against the Spirit."

This is a good place to mention that when we speak of the Holy Spirit as the third person of the Trinity, we are not saying that he is third in rank or divinity. It is simply that the Spirit is usually mentioned third when the persons of the Trinity are named, as in Matthew 28:19 (the institution of Baptism) and 2 Corinthians 13:14 (the apostolic blessing). There also is a natural order or relation of origin, with the Father as the first person, the Son as the second person, and the Holy Spirit as the third person, since the Son is begotten of the Father and the Spirit proceeds from the Father and the Son.

Jehovah's Witnesses speak of the Holy Spirit not as a person but as "God's 'active force'; the energy used by God to create the universe and to monitor and bless his creation."[27] Joseph Franklin Rutherford (1869–1942), founder of the sect, wrote in *The Harp of God*: "The holy spirit [sic] is the invisible power and energy of Jehovah."[28] Unitarians do not regard the Spirit as a separate person of the Godhead. Friedrich Schleiermacher, "the father of modern theology," taught that "the expression 'Holy Spirit' must be understood to mean the vital unity of the Christian fellowship as a moral personality; and this . . . we might denote by the phrase, *its common spirit*."[29]

The Council of Constantinople (381) and our Nicene Creed

There was another problem to clear up. In an attempt to explain how the divine and human natures were joined in Christ, Apollinaris of Laodicea had inadvertently denied the Savior's complete humanity. First, he said that the divine Logos (the Word) took the place of the human mind or soul in Jesus. When it was pointed out that this deprived the Son of his full humanity, Apollinaris changed his view and said that the Holy Spirit replaced the human spirit in Jesus. That, of course, still deprived Christ of his full humanity. Apollinaris was trying to explain how the great miracle of the union of the human and divine natures in Christ came about, a mystery that cannot be explained. Gregory of Nazianz made clear why the full and true humanity of Christ is a very important issue: "That which he has not assumed he has not healed."[30] It took a divine Savior with a totally human nature to rescue us human beings body and soul.

Contemporary with Apollinaris was Marcellus of Ancyra (modern Ankara, the capital of Turkey). He said that the one God expanded to three gods for the work of creation and redemption, and then contracted to one God again—a variation of modalism.

To deal with these continuing problems, co-emperors Theodosius I and Valentinian II convoked what history calls the Second Ecumenical Council. The bishops of the eastern part of the Roman Empire met in Constantinople in 381. The purpose of the council was to deal with the errors of the Pneumatomachians, Apollinaris, and Marcellus. No western bishops were invited, mostly because the West was not involved in any of the contemporary controversies. It was also the stated purpose of this synod to reaffirm the trinitarian faith confessed at Nicaea. For that purpose the assembled bishops discussed and finally adopted the revised Creed of Jerusalem that Athanasius and the Cappadocians had agreed upon at Alexandria in 362.

The council adopted the confession known to us as the Nicene Creed. Historians remember it as the Niceno-Constantinopolitan Creed or the Creed of Constantinople. We can summarize the trinitarian doctrine and the creed of that council in this way: (1) God is one being (*ousia*) in three persons (*hypostaseis*, he-PUH-stah-zice). (2) The Son and the Holy Spirit are of the same being (*homoousios*) as the Father.

Trinitarian Christianity became the only legally protected religion in the Roman Empire. This was not, as some have claimed, a victory of abstract Greek ideas over the more concrete message of the Bible's Jewish authors. Rather, the Nicene Creed put limits on Greek philosophical speculation regarding the triune God.

10

Modern Anti-Trinitarian Errors

Unitarianism

Arianism has reappeared at various times under various names and is still on the religious scene today. In 1531, the Spanish physician Miguel Servetus (Serv-EE-tus) published *On the Errors of the Trinity*. In it he not only attacked the doctrine of the Trinity but also assailed the teaching that in Christ the divine and human natures are united in one person. After his execution in Geneva in 1553, many who agreed with him found refuge in Poland. There they attached themselves to the followers of Faustus Socinus (So-SEEN-us, d. 1604), an Italian religious leader.

Socinus denied the Trinity and the deity of Christ. He said that Jesus was born of the virgin but denied that he is divine. In Socinus' view, Jesus was merely endowed with divine wisdom, power, and immortality. He came to proclaim God's forgiveness but did not win that forgiveness by making satisfaction for our sins. Persecuted for some years and finally forced out of Poland in 1658, some of the Socinians settled in Transylvania (today part of Romania). There, for the first time, people of Arian persuasion were called Unitarians.

In the 19th century the spiritual descendants of the Socinians declared agreement and fellowship with Unitarian groups in Great Britain and North America. In the United States the Unitarian Universalist Association is frank in its rejection of the Trinity—as well as the incarnation and the vicarious atonement. At least some Quakers have followed William Penn in rejecting the doctrine of the Trinity as it is confessed in the Nicene Creed and the Athanasian Creed.

Servetus, Socinus, and even 19th-century Unitarians misinterpreted the Bible in presenting and defending their views. Today Unitarians rely almost exclusively on the authority of human reason.

In the United States, the Evangelical and Reformed Church and the Congregational Christian Churches merged in 1957 to form the United Church of Christ. Some of the Congregational churches had earlier been part of the General Convention of Christian Churches, a nontrinitarian body. In the merge of 1957, these Congregational churches were not required to affirm the doctrine of the Trinity. Thus, the United Church of Christ is comprised of churches that confess the Trinity and others that do not.

There are many religious groups that follow Arius' basic teaching that Jesus Christ is not the eternal God become flesh but a mere human being. They may not follow Arius' doctrines in detail, but they share his basic error. The best known and most numerous representatives of Arianism today are Jehovah's Witnesses, officially known as the Watch Tower Bible and Tract Society, Inc. Jehovah's Witnesses formally acknowledge the Bible's authority, but they teach an Arian Christ on the basis of their New World Translation of the Bible and their clever manipulation of Scripture passages. They teach that Jesus had a beginning as the created Son of God. They delight in pointing out that the most obvious trinitarian statement in the King James Version of the Bible is not an authentic part of Holy Scripture. In the King James Version, 1 John 5:7 reads, "For there are three that bear record in heaven, the Father, the Word, and the Holy Ghost: and these three are one." What this verse says is true, as we know from many clear passages of Scripture, but it must not be regarded as part of the inspired Word of God. No Greek manuscript from before 1520 contains this verse.

Liberal Protestantism

It has been said, and it can hardly be disputed, that the public image, the general view of God, is today more unitarian than trinitarian. That is not so much because people have thought the doctrine through as because they are ignorant or indifferent in religious matters. Unitarians are less responsible for this state of affairs than are liberal theologians and preachers in nominally trinitarian churches. There are many liberal Protestants today who bear the name Christian and preach in churches that are officially trinitarian. Yet, they regard the Bible's teaching of the incarnation as myth. They tend to give the Son even less of the divine nature than Arius did. Naturally, then, they reject the doctrine of the Trinity—in fact, if not officially.

Deism and Freemasonry

The religion of many of the founding fathers of the United States of America was Deism. They followed the teachings of Lord Herbert of Cherbury, published in 1624. In summary, he taught that there is a Supreme Being, who created the universe but no longer involves himself in controlling it. It is as though God made a clock and simply lets it run. The word *Deism* derives from the Latin *deus* (DEH-us), meaning "god." Cherbury's god is to be worshiped but such worship consists mostly in piety and moral living. Sins are to be atoned for by repenting and making amends. Although God is not directly involved in the universe he created, he will punish or reward people after death, according to what they have done in their lifetimes. The founders and developers of Freemasonry were Deists, who carefully omitted references to Christ in their rituals. This accorded with their deistic belief that Christ is not to be thought of or worshiped as God.

Judaism

It might seem strange to mention Judaism here, but let us remember that Jesus and the authors of the New Testament were Jews. Moreover, we have seen that there are many evidences of the Trinity in the Old Testament. Of course, Jews who believe that Jesus is the promised Messiah are Christians. They might continue some of the traditional practices of their ancestors, but they are no longer adherents of Judaism. Nor do their families or other Jews regard them as authentic Jews.

Those Jews who still believe that God will send a Messiah generally believe that he will come as a man born of two human parents, and that his existence will begin then. That is, they do not believe that the Messiah will be the eternal or preexistent Son of God. It goes without saying that they do not believe the Christian doctrine of the Trinity.

Tritheism, polytheism, New Age religion, and pantheism

Tritheism is the teaching that there are three gods. Joseph Smith, Jr., the founder of Mormonism, said in a discourse of June 16, 1844: "I have always declared God to be a distinct personage, Jesus Christ as separate and distinct personage from God the Father, and the Holy Ghost as a distinct personage and a Spirit, and these three constitute three distinct personages and *three Gods* (emphasis added)."[31]

Polytheism is the teaching that there are many gods. Mormon theologians have claimed that in addition to the Father, Son, and Holy Spirit, "there can be, and are other Gods"[32] Thus, from two different official Mormon sources, we have both the doctrine of three gods (tritheism) and the doctrine of many gods (polytheism).

One of the best known teachings of Mormonism is the familiar "As man is, God once was; as God is, man may become." The official authority for this popular saying is found in the *Journal of Discourses*, Volume VI, page 3: "God was once as we are now, and is an exalted man."[33] The way to become a god is to obey the laws of the Church of Jesus Christ of Latter-day Saints.

A new kind of polytheism can be discerned in some forms of New Age religion. Some adherents boldly declare that all human beings are gods or have the potential to become gods. They urge people to elevate themselves to the dignity and the autonomy of gods. Their message is remarkably like that of the tempter in the Garden of Eden: God knows that when you deny him and depart from biblical and historic Christianity your eyes will be opened, and you will be gods.

Pantheism confuses the creation with its Creator. It says that everything is God and that there is no personal God above or apart from nature. There are strong elements of pantheism in the New Age Movement. John Schuetze writes:

> In his book *Unmasking the New Age*, Douglas R. Groothuis offers the following six statements to summarize the New Age:
>
> 1. ALL IS ONE—Groothuis explains: "Ultimately there is no difference between God, a person, a carrot, or a rock. They are all part of one continuous reality that has no boundaries, no ultimate division."
>
> 2. ALL IS GOD—The New Age teaches that God is everything and everything is god. God is not regarded as a personal being but an impersonal energy force. Everything that exists is god. This concept was evident in the Star Wars films with the presence of "the Force."
>
> 3. WE ARE ALL GOD—Since everything is god, it follows that we are all gods. The key is to awaken the god within us. A noted New Age leader urges: "Kneel to your own self. Honor and worship your own being. God dwells within you as you!"
>
> 4. A CHANGE OF CONSCIOUSNESS—Even though we are all gods, we don't know it. The problem is our ignorance, which keeps us from realizing

our divinity. The solution is enlightenment. Through meditation we can alter our consciousness and open the door to reality.

5. ALL RELIGIONS ARE ONE—Religions are simply different paths to the one truth. Thus the New Age seeks to incorporate all religions into its movement. Christianity is no exception. Rather than being the Savior of the world, they say Christ's mission was to alert the sleeping masses to their innate divinity.

6. NEW AGE COMING—The old age is passing away. A new age is dawning. We are part of a great transformation of consciousness and culture. Through "conscious evolution" we will be able to steer the cosmic ship into bigger and better times. New Agers call this the Age of Aquarius. According to astrology, this will happen when the sun begins to rise in Aquarius on the first day of spring. This will bring an end to the old age of Pisces, the fish, which some identify with the Christian era, since the fish was adopted as a symbol of Christianity. It will be replaced by the new Age of Aquarius, which will include a new world order, universal peace, and a completely different set of values. But because the various boundaries of the zodiac are so poorly defined, astrologers do not agree on when this Age of Aquarius will begin.[34]

Rosicrucianism

By no means a mass movement or a popular religion, Rosicrucianism nevertheless appeals to a certain class of people. It teaches that the Deity is one impersonal being composed of seven spirits and that it is manifested as a triune godhead. The Father is the highest initiate of the planet Saturn, the Son is the highest initiate of the sun, and the Holy Spirit is the highest initiate of the moon.

The man Jesus is the Son of God, or Christ, but he is only one member of a group that includes Buddha. The cross of the Ancient and Mystical Order of the Rose Cross—the Rosicrucian Fellowship—has no connection with the redemption of sinners. Rather, it is the sign of man's evolutionary past and his future destiny. Man is at this time a sort of demigod, evolving into a divine being. Jesus manifested himself in order to aid mankind in this evolutionary struggle.

A *female deity*

Among the most ancient of religions is the worship of a female deity, usually in connection with fertility rites. Isis in Egypt, Asherah among the Canaanites, and the Great Mother of Asia Minor are examples. Some modern feminists have adopted the worship of a female deity. Some have conceived of the earth itself as a female force with the name Gaia (GUY-ah).

Others, who want to remain Christian, have chosen to refer to the God of the Bible as Mother or she, rather than Father and he. Some regard the Holy Spirit as the female principle, or feminine aspect of God. These ideas, of course, contradict the plain language of the Bible. The "masculinity" of God is part of his self-revelation, recorded in the inspired Scriptures, and not something invented and imposed by patriarchal tradition.

11

We Believe: Creeds and Confessions

Creeds unite and divide

The gospel unites believers in Christ. The gospel also divides those who reject it from those who believe. The same is true of creeds. When Christians agree on a summary of the gospel as their confession of faith, they are saying, "We are united in the truth of God's Word." Those who disagree will be separated, or separate themselves, from those who share this confession of faith.

There are three ecumenical (universal) creeds. They summarize the church's doctrine of the triune God and his mighty acts. They also reject—implicitly in the Apostles' Creed, more explicitly in the Nicene and Athanasian

Creeds—ancient errors concerning God. As we have seen in the previous chapters, those ancient errors reappear from time to time in new forms with modern names. Although not all believers know them and not all churches officially recognize them, all Christians believe what the three ecumenical creeds teach.

There may be the danger that some people imagine they have fully comprehended God when they have come to understand a creed. There is always a danger that people will confuse knowing the right creed with trust in the God of our salvation, even imagining that they are saved just because they adhere to the "right" creed. Nevertheless, creeds are very useful in the life of the church as a standard for teaching and as a way of forestalling or correcting error. In the context of worship or of private devotion, they provide an opportunity for reviewing in brief the wonderful things God has done and is doing for the salvation of sinners and the welfare of his church. Whenever the writers of the New Testament summarize the work of Jesus or make statements about who he is, they are doing just what the creeds do in the Second Article. Putting it in another way, the Second Article in the ecumenical creeds summarizes Christ's work of redemption according to the New Testament record.

Early developments

After the time of the apostles, after the New Testament had been completed, Christians at various places and for various reasons found it useful to use short summaries of what the Bible teaches about God and his salvation. In order to give an answer to those who inquired about the Christian faith, in order to instruct those who wanted to be baptized, and in order to correct false teaching, churches in various localities added words and phrases as needed. The use of three articles in each of the creeds developed naturally from the baptismal formula "baptizing them in the name of the Father and of the Son and of the Holy Spirit" (Matthew 28:19). Before being baptized, converts were asked, "Do you believe in God the Father?" "Do you believe in God the Son?" "Do you believe in God the Holy Spirit?" The candidates for Baptism simply answered, "Yes," but then also briefly stated *what* they believed about each person.

The "Rule of Faith"

The exact wording of these brief confessions varied from place to place, but there was agreement in teaching. In the second century, Christians spoke of the "rule of faith," or the "canon (standard, norm) of truth." They were not referring to a set form of creed that all used. They were referring to the content of their various local statements of faith, all of which were in essential agreement with one another. In the Eastern church they usually began, "We believe," as a united confession of the church in that place. In the Western church they more often began, "I believe," as the personal confession of the individual, especially at the time of Baptism. It is from the Latin for the phrase "I believe" (*credo*, KRAY-doe), that our word *creed* comes. These early creeds, like creeds throughout the history of the church, were used for instructing those who sought to be baptized.

As time went on and Gnosticism, Monarchianism, and other errors threatened the church from the inside, the creeds became more detailed. They specified just who is meant by God the Father, who Jesus Christ is and what he did, and what the church is.

One of the local creeds was the so-called Old Roman Symbol, dated no later than 200, perhaps already in use around 150. The word *symbol* comes from the Greek word used in the Roman legions, meaning "password" or "watchword." Just as Roman soldiers recognized one another by their *symbolum*, so Christians recognize one another by their symbols (creeds and confessions).

The following form of the Old Roman Symbol will not seem entirely new or appear strange to most readers:

> I believe in God the Father almighty;
> And in Jesus Christ, his only Son, our Lord;
> Who was born by the Holy Spirit and the Virgin Mary,
> Who under Pontius Pilate was crucified and buried,
> on the third day he rose again from the dead,
>> ascended into heaven,
>> sits on the right hand of the Father,
>>> whence he will come to judge the living
>>> and the dead;
> and in the Holy Spirit,
>> the holy church,
>> the remission of sins,
>> the resurrection of the flesh.[35]

The Old Roman Symbol was obviously the forerunner of the Apostles' Creed. It is not known just when the Apostles' Creed was completed in the form in which we know it. Because it is briefer than the later creeds, because it has fewer abstract expressions, and because it summarizes the teaching of the person and work of Christ in concrete and biblical language, Martin Luther called it the children's creed.

> I believe in God, the Father almighty,
>> maker of heaven and earth.

I believe in Jesus Christ, his only Son, our Lord,
  who was conceived by the Holy Spirit,
  born of the virgin Mary,
  suffered under Pontius Pilate,
  was crucified, died, and was buried.
He descended into hell.
The third day he rose again from the dead.
He ascended into heaven
      and is seated at the right hand of God
        the Father almighty.
From there he will come to judge the living and the dead.
I believe in the Holy Spirit,
  the holy Christian Church,
    the communion of saints,
    the forgiveness of sins,
    the resurrection of the body,
    and the life everlasting. Amen.[36]

Like the other ecumenical creeds, this creed is tripartite, confessing faith in each person of the Trinity in a separate article. It does not treat the persons as impersonal "modes" or manifestations. Notice that gnostic ideas about where the world came from are addressed with the Bible-based confession that almighty God created it. "Father almighty" declares that God is still actively involved in governing his creation.

Notice that Jesus Christ is acknowledged as truly divine, but that the creed emphasizes his true humanity by summarizing his earthly career. His virgin mother is named and his place in historical time is documented by the mention of the governor who ordered his execution.

If the twelve apostles had written the Apostles' Creed, as legend said they did, there would have been no need for the Old Roman Symbol, which came in the century after the apostles' ministry. The Apostles' Creed is really a later development of the Old Roman Symbol. Another reason we know that the Apostles' Creed was not actually composed by the apostles is that the Eastern church never used it in the form we are familiar with. The churches of the East (Greek, Syrian, Egyptian, Chaldean, etc.) produced their own confessions, similar in content and form to the creed of the West but not exactly the same in wording. Those creeds and the Old Roman Symbol were quite fully developed by the year 200. Of course, the words and phrases in them can be traced back to the earliest Christian literature, the New Testament itself.

For that very reason the Apostles' Creed is apostolic in the sense that it teaches what the apostles taught. It is apostolic because it agrees with what the apostles wrote by inspiration of the Holy Spirit.

The Nicene Creed

We have seen that the Council of Nicaea (325) answered the question "Is Jesus Christ God or not?" The answer was "Yes, he is *homoousios* with (of the same being as) the Father. Whatever is true of the Father is true of the Son according to this divine nature—but the Son is not the Father." The argument continued for 56 years, until the Council of Constantinople (381). The creed adopted at Constantinople, based on the Creed of Jerusalem, came to be called the Nicene Creed because it faithfully expresses what the church confessed at Nicaea in 325. Historians also know it as the Niceno-Constantinopolitan Creed, or the Constantinopolitan Symbol.

In 451 the Council of Chalcedon (KAL-si-dun) formally adopted what we call the Nicene Creed for use in all the churches, and it soon became part of the liturgy. We could say that this creed is more "ecumenical" than the

Apostles' Creed and the Athanasian Creed in the sense
that the Eastern Orthodox Church has never used the latter two in its liturgies, although it accepts their content.

> We believe in one God, the Father, the Almighty,
>> maker of heaven and earth,
>> of all that is,
>> seen and unseen.
> We believe in one Lord, Jesus Christ, the only Son
>> of God,
>> eternally begotten of the Father,
>> God from God, Light from Light, true God
>>> from true God,
>> begotten, not made,
>> of one being with the Father.
> Through him all things were made.
> For us and for our salvation, he came down from heaven,
>> was incarnate of the Holy Spirit and the virgin Mary,
>> and became fully human.
> For our sake he was crucified under Pontius Pilate.
> He suffered death and was buried.
> On the third day he rose again in accordance with
>> the Scriptures.
> He ascended into heaven
>> and is seated at the right hand of the Father.
> He will come again in glory to judge the living and
>> the dead,
>> and his kingdom will have no end.
> We believe in the Holy Spirit,
>> the Lord, the giver of life,
>> who proceeds from the Father and the Son,
>> who in unity with the Father and the Son is
>>> worshiped and glorified,
>> who has spoken through the prophets.
> We believe in one holy Christian and apostolic Church.
> We acknowledge one baptism for the forgiveness of sins.
> We look for the resurrection of the dead
>> and the life of the world to come. Amen.[37]

Notice that, like the Apostles' Creed, the Nicene Creed speaks of what God has done in history and is doing in time for our salvation. Notice, however, that it *also* speaks of who God *is eternally.* "One Lord, Jesus Christ" says that he is the only Savior of this world. "Of one being with the Father"—in older English versions "of one substance with the Father"—expresses the *homoousios* for which Athanasius so heroically contended.

The difficult concept *begotten* as applied to the Son, who is eternal, is made clear with the expression "not made." As the "eternally begotten of the Father," he is "God, . . . Light, . . . true God." And yet, "he became fully human." The mystery of how God and man are joined in one person is as profound as the mystery of the Trinity. Had the incarnation—the union of the divine and human in Christ—not occurred, we would not know about or be interested in the Trinity. It did occur, and we believe that all he did was "for us and for our salvation," "for our sake."

Recall that the Third Article in the Creed of Nicaea (325) simply said, "and in the Holy Spirit." In part because of attacks on the personality and especially on the deity of the Holy Spirit, that very brief Third Article was expanded at the Council of Constantinople (381). Our Nicene Creed acknowledges the Spirit's creative work with the words "the Lord and giver of life." It also relates the Spirit to the Father and the Son by confessing that the Spirit proceeds from both of them. Because he is God and because of his work on our behalf, he "is worshiped and glorified." The article also takes note of his particular work: He "has spoken through the prophets," also foretelling that Christ would rise again on the third day, "in accordance with the Scriptures."

The Athanasian Creed

Like the other two ecumenical creeds, this confession of faith is also misnamed. The Apostles' Creed confesses the teachings of the apostles, but they did not write it. The Nicene Creed confesses the teaching of the Council of Nicaea, but it was actually adopted at the Council of Constantinople. The Athanasian Creed confesses the teachings of Athanasius, and in even more detail, but he did not write it.

Athanasius' working language was Greek, but the creed named for him was written in Latin. Neither he nor those who wrote in praise of him after his death made any mention of this document. Athanasius was a theologian of the East, but the creed (written in Latin, remember) was not even known in the Greek Orthodox Church until about 1200. Some of the thoughts and expressions in the creed, regarding the relationship of the divine to the human in Christ, had not been formulated at the time Athanasius died (373). Many of the thoughts and expressions bear a striking resemblance to the language of the Definition of the Faith of Chalcedon (451). The creed also includes a clear summary of what was confessed at Nicaea (325) and Constantinople (381). Because it begins with the Latin word *quicunque* (quee-KUN-kweh, "whoever"), it is also known as the *Symbolum Quicunque*—The Whoever Confession.

Who did write this creed, then? No one is certain. Some say a learned monk in southern Gaul (modern France). Others say a learned monk in southern Spain. The date is also uncertain, but it must have been after 451 (Council of Chalcedon) and probably before 600. Since it is arranged so artistically and is so rhythmic, it was probably intended for chanting. It was, in fact, sung daily in the monastic liturgical service called Prime from before the year 800:

> Whoever *(Quicunque)* wishes to be saved must, above all else, hold to the true Christian faith.
>> Whoever does not keep this faith pure in all points will certainly perish forever.
> Now this is the true Christian faith:
> We worship one God in three persons and three persons in one God,
>> without mixing the persons or dividing the divine being.
> For each person—the Father, the Son, and the Holy Spirit—is distinct,
>> but the deity of Father, Son, and Holy Spirit is one, equal in glory and coeternal in majesty.
> What the Father is, so is the Son, and so is the Holy Spirit.
> The Father is uncreated, the Son uncreated, the Holy Spirit uncreated;
> the Father is infinite, the Son infinite, the Holy Spirit infinite;
> the Father is eternal, the Son is eternal, the Holy Spirit is eternal;
>> yet they are not three who are eternal, but there is one who is eternal,
>> just as they are not three who are uncreated, nor three who are infinite,
>> but there is one who is uncreated and one who is infinite.
> In the same way the Father is almighty, the Son is almighty, the Holy Spirit is almighty;
>> yet they are not three who are almighty, but there is one who is almighty.
> So the Father is God, the Son is God, the Holy Spirit is God;
>> yet they are not three Gods, but one God.

So the Father is Lord, the Son is Lord, the Holy Spirit
    is Lord;
  yet they are not three Lords, but one Lord.
For just as Christian truth compels us to confess each
        person individually to be God and Lord,
    so the true Christian faith forbids us to speak of
        three Gods or three Lords.
The Father is neither made nor created nor begotten
    of anyone.
The Son is neither made nor created, but is begotten of
    the Father alone.
The Holy Spirit is neither made nor created nor begotten,
but proceeds from the Father and the Son.
  So there is one Father, not three Fathers; one Son,
        not three Sons;
    one Holy Spirit, not three Holy Spirits.
And within this Trinity none comes before or after; none
    is greater or inferior,
  but all three persons are coequal and coeternal,
so that in every way, as stated before, all three persons are
        to be worshiped as one God and one God
        worshiped as three persons.
  Whoever wishes to be saved must have this
        conviction of the Trinity.
It is furthermore necessary for eternal salvation truly
    to believe
that our Lord Jesus Christ also took on human flesh.
Now this is the true Christian faith:
  We believe and confess that our Lord Jesus Christ,
        God's Son,
    is both God and man.
He is God, eternally begotten from the nature of the
        Father, and he is man, born in time from the
        nature of his mother, fully God, fully man, with
        rational soul and human flesh,
    equal to the Father as to his deity, less than the
        Father as to his humanity;

and though he is both God and man, Christ is not two
persons but one,
one, not by changing the deity into flesh, but by
taking the humanity into God;
one, indeed, not by mixture of the natures, but by unity in
one person;
for just as the rational soul and flesh are one human
being,
so God and man are one Christ.
He suffered for our salvation, descended into hell, rose the
third day from the dead.
He ascended into heaven, is seated at the right hand
of God the Father almighty, and from there
will come to judge the living and the dead.
At his coming all people will rise with their own bodies
to answer for their personal deeds.
Those who have done good will enter eternal life,
but those who have done evil will go into
eternal fire.
This is the true Christian faith.
Whoever does not faithfully and firmly believe this
cannot be saved.[38]

Notice that this creed divides itself into two major
parts. The first concerns the Trinity and the Unity of God.
The second concerns itself with the person and natures of
Christ. The creed addresses and confesses these two doctrines in a more complete and precise manner than do the
other two ecumenical creeds.

In part because of its length, the creed is not used for
public worship on a regular basis. In some churches it is
not used at all. In some it is used each year on Trinity Sunday. Apart from any doctrinal concerns or reservations
they may have, critics have taken issue with the first two
and the last two sentences of the creed. Let us consider
whether the criticism is justified.

"Whoever wishes to be saved must, above all else, hold to the true Christian faith. Whoever does not keep this faith pure in all points will certainly perish forever." Critics say that here faith as trust in the Savior is being confused with a particular exposition or expression of the faith. We respond that there can be no saving faith, no trust in God and his salvation, without faith's object. Faith must rest on something—really someone—and that someone and his saving work are thoroughly described in this creed. Like the other two ecumenical creeds, and in a much more thorough way than they do, this creed summarizes the gospel, without which there can be no true faith. Knowledge of the triune God, the divine Christ, and Christ's work of redemption are fundamental to faith.

"This is the true Christian faith. Whoever does not faithfully and firmly believe this cannot be saved." Doesn't that make conformity with a set form of words necessary for salvation? What about people who don't know this creed or who lack a clear understanding of it? Wayne Schulz has answered the objections very well: "Of course, it is not necessary for salvation to know the Athanasian Creed or to be conversant with its theology. On the other hand, anyone who is fully acquainted with its testimony yet denigrates or denies what it teaches about the Christian God and the Christian Savior has suffered shipwreck of the true Christian faith."[39]

Ours is an age in which many people believe that all religions lead to the same God. It must be stressed that according to the Bible, it is necessary to believe in the triune God to be saved. If one does not believe in Christ and worship him along with the Father, one is not worshiping the true God. God's Word says, "No one who denies the Son has the Father; whoever acknowledges the Son has the Father also" (1 John 2:23). "Anyone who runs ahead and does not continue in the teaching of Christ does not have God; whoever continues in the teaching has both the Father and the Son" (2 John 9).

Martin Luther's catechisms

Lutherans include Martin Luther's Small Catechism and Large Catechism among their confessional writings. In his Small Catechism, Luther briefly explained the Apostles' Creed, article by article. For any reader who may not be familiar with that writing, we quote from it here.[40]

THE FIRST ARTICLE
(Creation)

I believe in God the Father almighty, maker of heaven and earth.

What does this mean?

I believe that God created me and all that exists, and that he gave me my body and soul, eyes, ears, and all my members, my mind and all my abilities.

And I believe that God still preserves me by richly and daily providing clothing and shoes, food and drink, property and home, spouse and children, land, cattle, and all I own, and all I need to keep my body and life. God also preserves me by defending me against all danger, guarding and protecting me from all evil. All this God does only because he is my good and merciful Father in heaven, and not because I have earned or deserved it. For all this I ought to thank and praise, to serve and obey him.

This is most certainly true.

THE SECOND ARTICLE
(Redemption)

I believe in Jesus Christ, his only Son, our Lord, who was conceived by the Holy Spirit, born of the virgin Mary, suffered under Pontius Pilate, was crucified, died, and was buried. He descended into hell. The third day he rose again from the dead. He ascended into heaven and is seated at the right hand of God the Father almighty. From there he will come to judge the living and the dead.

What does this mean?

I believe that Jesus Christ, true God, begotten of the Father from eternity, and also true man, born of the virgin Mary, is my Lord.

He has redeemed me, a lost and condemned creature, purchased and won me from all sins, from death, and from the power of the devil, not with gold or silver but with his holy, precious blood and with his innocent suffering and death.

All this he did that I should be his own, and live under him in his kingdom, and serve him in everlasting righteousness, innocence, and blessedness, just as he has risen from death and lives and rules eternally.

This is most certainly true.

THE THIRD ARTICLE
(Sanctification)

I believe in the Holy Spirit; the holy Christian church, the communion of saints; the forgiveness of sins; the resurrection of the body; and the life everlasting. Amen.

What does this mean?

I believe that I cannot by my own thinking or choosing believe in Jesus Christ, my Lord, or come to him.

But the Holy Spirit has called me by the gospel, enlightened me with his gifts, sanctified and kept me in the true faith. In the same way he calls, gathers, enlightens, and sanctifies the whole Christian church on earth, and keeps it with Jesus Christ in the one true faith.

In this Christian church he daily and fully forgives all sins to me and all believers.

On the Last Day he will raise me and all the dead and give eternal life to me and all believers in Christ.

This is most certainly true.

Luther prepared his Large Catechism as an aid for those who would teach the catechism in churches and schools. It confesses the same truths as those found in the Small Catechism, including the treatment of the Trinity in the Apostles' Creed but expounds them at greater length and in greater detail.

The Lutheran Confessions

The Lutheran Confessions, including Martin Luther's catechisms, are writings that present the standard teachings of the evangelical Lutheran church. They are the standard, the norm of doctrine, because they are a faithful presentation of what is taught in the Holy Scriptures. The Scriptures, of course, are the absolute standard, or norm, of teaching.

The Lutheran princes of Germany, with the help of their theologians, presented a confession of faith to Emperor Charles V at the Diet of Augsburg on June 25, 1530. Their

Augsburg Confession began by confessing the triune God. They wanted to make clear that they agreed with the whole Christian church on earth in this trinitarian faith. They also wanted to demonstrate that they were not "outlaws," for the law of the Holy Roman Empire made trinitarian Christianity the only legal religion of Germany.

Article I of the Augsburg Confession reads, in a translation of the German text:

> We unanimously hold and teach, in accordance with the decree of the Council of Nicaea, that there is one divine essence, which is called and which is truly God, and that there are three persons in this one divine essence, equal in power and alike eternal: God the Father, God the Son, God the Holy Spirit. All three are one divine essence, eternal, without division, without end, of infinite power, wisdom, and goodness, one creator and preserver of all things visible and invisible. The word "person" is to be understood as the Fathers employed the term in this connection, not as a part or a property of another, but as that which exists of itself.[41]

Because there was no disagreement with the Roman Catholic Church over the doctrine of the Trinity, the Apology (defense and explanation) of the Augsburg Confession does not elaborate much on Article I of the Augsburg Confession. In late 1536 and early 1537, Martin Luther himself prepared a confession of faith, the Smalcald Articles. This confession also begins with an affirmation of the Lutherans' trinitarian faith. While Article I of the Augsburg Confession emphasizes who God is, the Smalcald Articles recount more of what God has done. As we noted earlier, the Lutheran Formula of Concord (1577) also affirmed the Trinity and rejected the errors of certain anti-Trinitarians.

Much more can be said about the Bible's teaching on the Holy Trinity. It is the hope of the author that what has been included in this book will be helpful. Especially, the hope is that this study of the Trinity will make readers more sure of salvation in Christ and more thankful to the God of our salvation. Not in identical words, but with one heart and mind, the entire Christian church on earth prays, and we join in the prayer:

> Almighty God and Father, dwelling in majesty and mystery, filling and renewing all creation by your eternal Spirit, and manifesting your saving grace through our Lord Jesus Christ: in mercy cleanse our hearts and lips that, free from doubt and fear, we may ever worship you, one true immortal God, with your Son and the Holy Spirit, living and reigning, now and forever.[42]

Endnotes

[1]Friedrich Schleiermacher, *The Christian Faith*, translated and edited by H. R. Mackintosh and J. S. Stewart, Vol. 2 (New York: Harper & Row, 1963), p. 535.

[2]Lyle L. Luchterhand, *Man: From Glory to Ashes and Back*, The People's Bible Teachings (Milwaukee: Northwestern Publishing House, 1998), pp. 30,31.

[3]Martin Luther, *Luther's Works*, edited by Jaroslav Pelikan and Helmut T. Lehmann, American Edition, Vol. 23 (St. Louis: Concordia Publishing House; Philadelphia: Fortress Press, 1955–1986), p. 28.

[4]*Christian Worship: A Lutheran Hymnal* (Milwaukee: Northwestern Publishing House, 1993), p. 132.

[5]*Luther's Works*, Vol. 41, pp. 103,104.

[6]*Christian Worship*, p. 133.

[7]*Christian Worship*, p. 19.

[8]*Christian Worship*, pp. 48,49.

[9]Formula of Concord, Solid Declaration, Article XI:66, *The Book of Concord: The Confessions of the Evangelical Lutheran Church*, translated and edited by Theodore G. Tappert (Philadelphia: Fortress Press, 1959), p. 627.

[10]Athenagoras, *Embassy for the Christians*, in Ancient Christian Writers, Vol. 23 (Westminster, Maryland: Newman Press, 1956), p. 41.

[11]Origen, *On First Principles* 1.2.2, in Harper Torchbooks, The Cathedral Library (New York: Harper & Row, 1966), p. 16.

[12]Origen, *On First Principles* 2.4.2, in The Ante-Nicene Fathers, edited by Alexander Roberts and James Donaldson, Vol. 4 (Grand Rapids: William B. Eerdmans Publishing Company, reprinted 1989), p. 282.

[13]Augsburg Confession, Article I:2, Tappert, p. 27.

[14]Augsburg Confession, Article I:4, Tappert, p. 28.

[15]Saint Hilary of Poitiers, *The Trinity*, translated by Stephen McKenna (New York: Fathers of the Church, Inc., 1954), pp. 127,261,403.

[16]Saint Augustine, *The Trinity*, translated by Stephen McKenna (Washington, D.C.: The Catholic University of America Press, 1963), pp. 187,188.

[17]*The Meaning of the Glorious Koran: An Explanatory Translation*, introduction and notes by Muhammad Marmaduke Pickthall (Boston: Allen and Unwin, 1976), Part X, Surah ix, 30, p. 30.

[18]*The Glorious Koran*, Part VI, Surah iv, 171, p. 131.

[19]Tertullian, *Against Praxeas*, 3, in The Ante-Nicene Fathers, Vol. 3, pp. 598,599.

[20]R. C. H. Lenski, *The Interpretation of St. Matthew's Gospel* (Columbus, Ohio: Wartburg Press, 1943), p. 1177.

[21]Eusebius, *The History of the Church from Christ to Constantine*, translated by G. A. Williamson (Minneapolis: Augsburg Publishing House, 1975), p. 317.

[22]Formula of Concord, Epitome, Article XII:4, Tappert, p. 498.

[23]Athanasius, *Against the Arians, Discourse* 1.2.5, in A Select Library of Nicene and Post-Nicene Fathers of the Christian Church, Second Series, edited by Philip Schaff and Henry Wace (Grand Rapids: William B. Eerdmans Publishing Company, 1971), p. 308.

[24]Origen, *On First Principles* 1.2.2, in The Ante-Nicene Fathers, p. 246.

[25]Athanasius, *Contra Gentes, and De Incarnatione* (Against the Gentiles and Concerning the Incarnation), edited and translated by Robert W. Thomson (Oxford: Clarendon Press, 1971), p. 269.

[26]Socrates Scholasticus, *History of the Church* 1.8, in *A Source Book for Ancient Church History from the Apostolic Age to the Close of the Conciliar Period*, Joseph Cullen Ayer, Jr., (New York: Charles Scribner's Sons, 1952), p. 305.

[27]Heather and Gary Botting, *The Orwellian World of Jehovah's Witnesses* (Toronto: University of Toronto Press, 1984), p. 189.

[28]J. F. Rutherford, *The Harp of God* (Brooklyn, New York: Watch Tower Bible and Tract Society, Inc., 1921), p. 15.

[29]Schleiermacher, *The Christian Faith*, Vol. 2, p. 535.

[30]Gregory of Nazianzus, *Epistle 101*, in A Select Library of Nicene and Post-Nicene Fathers of the Christian Church, Second Series, Vol. 7, p. 440.

[31]Quoted in *Selections from Answers to Gospel Questions Taken from the Writings of Joseph Fielding Smith, Tenth President of the Church: A Course of Study for the Melchizedek Priesthood Quorums of the Church of Jesus Christ of Latter Day Saints 1972–73*, (Utah: Deseret News Press, 1972), p. 11.

[32]*Selections from Answers to Gospel Questions*, p. 13.

[33]Ed Decker and Dave Hunt, *The God Makers* (Eugene, Oregon: Harvest House Publishers, ca. 1984), p. 31.

[34]John D. Schuetze, *Angels and Demons: Have Wings—Will Travel*, The People's Bible Teachings (Milwaukee: Northwestern Publishing House, 1997), pp. 81-83.

[35]J. N. D. Kelly, *Early Christian Creeds* (New York: David McKay Company, Inc., 1972), p. 102.

[36]*Christian Worship*, p. 19.

[37]*Christian Worship*, pp. 18,19.

[38]*Christian Worship*, pp. 132,133.

[39]*Christian Worship: Manual*, edited by Gary Baumler and Kermit Moldenhauer (Milwaukee: Northwestern Publishing House, 1993), p. 222.

[40]*Luther's Catechism: The Small Catechism of Dr. Martin Luther and an Exposition for Children and Adults Written in Contemporary English*, by David P. Kuske (Milwaukee: Northwestern Publishing House, 3rd Edition, 1998), pp. 4,5.

[41]Augsburg Confession, Article I:1-4, Tappert, pp. 27,28.

[42]Prayer of the Day for Trinity Sunday, *Christian Worship: Manual*, p. 422.

For Further Reading

Caemmerer, R. R. "The Nature and Attributes of God." *The Abiding Word*. Vol. 2. St. Louis: Concordia Publishing House, 1947.

Essays in *Our Great Heritage*. 3 vols. Edited by Lyle W. Lange. Milwaukee: Northwestern Publishing House, 1991:

Meyer, John P. "The Holy Trinity." Vol. 1.

Meyer, John P. "Ancient Errors about God." Vol. 1.

"Modern Errors about God." Vol. 1.

    Winterstein, Herbert. "Unitarian Universalists."

    Kuehl, D. H. "Mormons."

    Beckmann, Walter. "Christian Science."

    Bergholz, H. W. "Unity."

    Schulz, Reuel. "Jehovah's Witnesses."

Reim, Edmund. "Ancient Heresies in Modern Garb—Errors Which Affect the Deity of Christ." Vol. 2.

Pieper, Francis. *Christian Dogmatics*. Vol. 1. St. Louis: Concordia Publishing House, 1950.

Scripture Index

10:9,13—24
10:13,14—21,22
10:17—29

1 Corinthians
2:10—50
2:11—11
3:16—50
8:4—78
12:3—29,68
12:6,11—50
12:11—52

2 Corinthians
8:9—98
13:14—49,66,69,106

Galatians
3:26—33
4:4—35
4:4,5—83
4:6—54,84

Ephesians
2:8,9—29
2:18—83
2:22—52,83
5:25,26—83
4:30—48

Philippians
1:19—54
2:6-8—97
2:9-12—43
3:21—38,39

Colossians
1:16—38,82
2:8,9—92
2:9—43,45
2:15—40

1 Timothy
6:16—11
6:20,21—92

2 Timothy
3:15-17—20

Titus
3:15—49

Hebrews
1:2,3—82
1:3—38
1:5—72
1:6—73
1:7-9—73,74
1:10-12—74
1:13—75
2:14—36
2:14,15—36
4:15—35
7:26—35
9:14—50

James
2:19—27

1 Peter
1:2—67
1:3—32,40,41

Subject Index

belief. *See* faith
Buddhism 18

Cappadocia 105
Carthage 94
catechisms 130-132
Charlemagne 53
Charles V (emperor) 132
Christian Science 93
Church of Jesus Christ of
     Latter-day Saints 93,
     113
compassionate (divine
     attribute) 27
Congregational Christian
     Churches 110
conscience 14,15,17,18
Constantine (emperor)
     101-103
Constantinopolitan Creed.
     See Nicene Creed
Constantinopolitan Symbol.
     See Nicene Creed
Council of Chalcedon 122
Council of Constantinople
     106-108,122,124
Council of Nicaea 101-103,
     122
creation 12,13,31,81,82
     and God the Holy Spirit
     51,82
     and God the Son 37,38,
     81,82
Creed of Constantinople. *See*
     Nicene Creed
Creed of Jerusalem 105,107,
     122

Creed of Nicaea 103,104
creeds
     development 117-119
     ecumenical 63,64
     misnaming 125

Darwin, Charles 17
Definition of the Faith of
     Chalcedon 125
Deism 112
Diet of Augsburg 132
Docetism 34,35,89
dynamism 96

Eastern Orthodox Church 54,
     123
Ebionites 88
Eddy, Mary Baker 93
Elkesaites 88
equilateral triangle 80
essence 77,104.
     See also being; *ousia*;
     substance
eternal (divine attribute) 25,
     43,44,50
Eunomius 104
Eusebius of Nicomedia 103
Evangelical and Reformed
     Church 110
evolution 17

faith 27-30
     rule of 119
Father. *See* God the Father
female deity 116
filioque 53-56
fleur-de-lis 80